ADHD Book: Living Right Now!

ADHD BOOK
Living Right Now!

Martin L. Kutscher, MD
Departments of Pediatrics and Neurology
New York Medical College, Valhalla, NY.
Pediatric Neurological Associates
White Plains, NY.

Neurology Press

125 South Broadway, White Plains, NY 10605

www.PediatricNeurology.com

Printed in the United States of America

ISBN 0-9740139-0-0

Library of Congress Control Number: 2003092320

Second Printing

Disclaimer: This text is provided as an educational resource. It does not constitute medical advice; nor is it a substitute for discussion between patients and their doctors.

To my wife,
whose constant attention to our family
continues to amaze me;

To my children,
whose very existence
is a miracle;

To the mothers of my patients,
who give unconditional love
to their children;

And to my patients,
who didn't choose to have the problems
that they cope with daily.

Table of Contents

Short on time?
First read the Summary Chapter 8, then the Home Chapter 2.

Introduction

The winners are
the parents whose child
still loves them when the child turns 18.

The purpose of this concise book is to be useful.

After all, there is a lot of work to be done. This thing we call "Attention Deficit Hyperactivity Disorder (ADHD)" is not just about cute, unfocused kids running around. If that were the only problem in your life, you would not be reading this. ADHD is often about overwhelmed kids who yell at their mother when she tries to help them. It is about mothers who fear that their relationship with their child is slipping away. It is about fathers who come home to find everyone at wit's end. It is about the threat to the most important things in life.

As I hear these stories over and over again in my practice in pediatric neurology, there are so many things I want to explain to families. I want to explain that the problems they are experiencing--the disorganization, the lack of planning, the living as if only the present moment exists, the over-reactions, the screaming, the lying, the blaming others, etc.-- are usually caused biologically as part of the condition we summarize with the letters ADHD. I want to explain behavioral approaches for home and school, and the role of medications.

I wanted a book that would concisely re-enforce it all. I made many recommendations for the truly excellent books that exist. However, most times, the parent's response at the next visit was, "No, Dr. Kutscher, I didn't read that yet. If I had time in my life to read all of those 300 page books you recommended, I wouldn't have needed them in the first place." Yet, the need existed. So, I scoured through the top books, condensed the best insights of brilliant thinkers, added some of my own, and wrote this text. The idea was to be brief, but not "dumbed down." Realistic, yet optimistic.

We begin with a discussion of the problems that we face: the full spectrum of ADHD and co-occurring symptoms. The chief difficulty is that people with ADHD cannot inhibit the present moment long enough to consider the future. ADHD behaviors make sense once we realize that they are based on reactions taking only the present moment into account. It is not that Johnny doesn't *care* about the future; it is that the future and the past don't even exist. Such is the nature of the disability. If you want to make sense out of inexplicable behaviors by someone with ADHD, just ask yourself: "What behavior makes sense if you only had 4 seconds left to live?" For example, if you only had 4 seconds to live, it *would* make sense to play a videogame rather than do homework. After all, why do homework if college doesn't exist?

The rest of the book deals with solutions. First, behavioral approaches for home and school are discussed. The key to therapy is recognition that ADHD is a true disability, which requires continuous "enabling" by parents and teachers—caregivers who need to constantly defuse (not inflame) an already overwhelming situation. Then, we move on to the role of medications. We end with a summary re-cap, which can be read as a complete freestanding text. The summary chapter could be provided to spouses, teachers, etc. Finally, a pop quiz and further readings are included.

I am indebted to the original thinkers who have added so much to this field. I have cited their works when possible. I am further indebted to those in my life who have added to my understanding of the full spectrum of ADHD. I hope that you find this book useful—and brief enough for you to actually read and use. The stakes are high: nothing less than our children's success, and our relationship with our children.

Good luck to your family. It will take time, but it *can* turn out great!

Martin L. Kutscher, M.D.
Departments of Pediatrics and Neurology
New York Medical College
Valhalla, New York

Pediatric Neurological Associates
125 South Broadway
White Plains, New York 10605

webmaster@www.PediatricNeurology.com

Chapter 1

The Problems:

More than We Expected

The ADHD Iceberg:
More Problems than We Expected

We've Been Missing the Point

> *"Johnny is very active! He never stops moving. He gets distracted by any little noise, and has the attention span of a flea. Often, he acts before he thinks. His sister, Jill, is often in a fog. Sometimes, she's just so spaced!"*

That is how we typically consider children with Attention Deficit Hyperactivity Disorder (ADHD). OK, not so bad. But that is often only the tip of the iceberg. Here is another likely description of the whole picture for a child with ADHD:

> *"I can't take it any more!! We scream all morning to get out of the house. Homework takes hours. If I don't help him with his work, he's so disorganized that he'll never do well. If I do help him, he screams at me. Since he never finishes anything, everyone thinks he doesn't care. No matter how much we beg or punish, he keeps doing the same stupid things over and over again. He never considers the consequences of his actions, and doesn't seem to care if they hurt me. It's so easy for him to get overwhelmed. Sometimes, he just wants to 'turn the noise off.' He is so inflexible, and then blows up over anything. It gets me so angry that I scream back, which makes everything even worse. Now that he's getting older, the lies and the cursing are getting worse, too. I know he has trouble paying attention, but why does he have all of these other problems as well?"*

It is not a coincidence that children with ADHD often manifest so much more than the classic triad of inattention, impulsivity, and hyperactivity. When we focus merely on these typically defined symptoms, we fail to deal with the whole vista of difficult problems experienced by patients and their families. This spectrum includes a wide range of "executive dysfunction" (such as poor self-control and foresight), additional co-occurring disorders (such as anxiety, depression or conduct disorders), and family stresses. These are summarized graphically in the first figure.

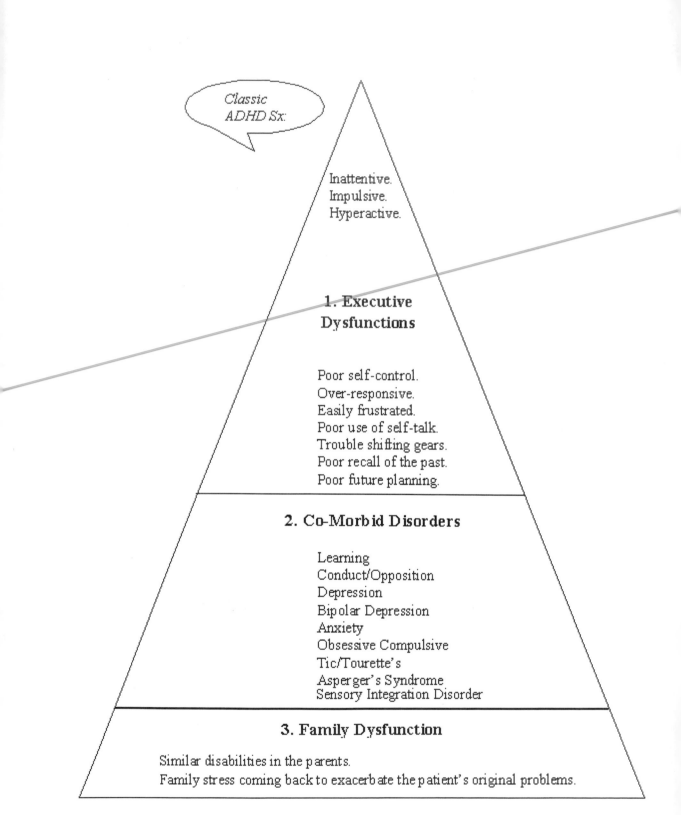

Classic
ADHD Sx:

Inattentive.
Impulsive.
Hyperactive.

1. Executive Dysfunctions

Poor self-control.
Over-responsive.
Easily frustrated.
Poor use of self-talk.
Trouble shifting gears.
Poor recall of the past.
Poor future planning.

2. Co-Morbid Disorders

Learning
Conduct/Opposition
Depression
Bipolar Depression
Anxiety
Obsessive Compulsive
Tic/Tourette's
Asperger's Syndrome
Sensory Integration Disorder

3. Family Dysfunction

Similar disabilities in the parents.
Family stress coming back to exacerbate the patient's original problems.

Redefining ADHD to Include "Executive Dysfunction"

ADHD needs to be redefined to include a wide range of "executive dysfunction." As Russell Barkley explains (see Resources), this dysfunction stems from an inability to inhibit present behavior so that demands for the future can be met.

So, what are Executive Functions?

When you step on a snake, it bites. No verbal discussion occurs within the snake's brain. No recall of whether striking back worked in the past. No thought as to where this action will lead in the future. No inhibition. Stepped on. Bite back. Humans, fortunately, have the option to modulate their behavior.

No single part of the human brain is solely in charge of this modulation. It does appear, however, that our frontal and pre-frontal lobes function largely as our "Chief Executive Officer (CEO)." Orchestrating language and memory functions from other parts of the brain, these frontal centers consider where we came from, where we want to go--and how to control ourselves in order to get there.

Most importantly, the ability to inhibit ("putting on the brakes") is central to effective executive function. Successful execution of a plan largely involves putting brakes on distracting activities. These brakes--courtesy of our pre-frontal inhibitory centers--allow us the luxury of time during which we can consider our options before reacting.

This lack of inhibition is a double problem for people with ADHD. First, without these brakes, they will be viewed as unable to adequately inhibit distractions, inhibit impulsive reactions, or inhibit physically acting upon these stimuli (hyperactivity). Second, patients with ADHD do not inhibit their behavior long enough for the *other* executive functions below to adequately develop either. Executive functions identified by Barkley include:

Self-talk refers to the ability to talk to ourselves--a mechanism by which we work through our choices using words. Toddlers can be heard using self-talk out loud. Eventually, this ability becomes internalized and automatic. However, ADHD patients have not inhibited their reactions long enough for this skill to fully develop.

Working memory refers to those ideas that we can keep active in our minds at a given moment. For example, in order to learn from mistakes, you have to be able to juggle

7

not just the present situation, but also keep in mind past times when certain strategies did or did not work. Working memory hopefully also includes keeping future goals in mind (such as remembering that we want to get into a good college, not just do the most intriguing activity currently available). Without the ability to inhibit, people with ADHD never get to develop good function of their working memory.

Foresight (predicting and planning for the future) will be deficient when inadequate working memory teams up with a poor ability to inhibit the present distractions. People with ADHD cannot keep the future in mind. They are prisoners of the present; the future catches them off guard. In fact, surprisingly poor foresight is perhaps the greatest difficulty in their lives.

Sense of time is an executive function that is usually extremely poor in ADHD.

Shifting from Agenda A to Agenda B is a difficult task requiring good executive function. Pulling yourself out of one activity and switching to another--transitioning-- is innately difficult, and requires effort and control.

Separating emotion from fact requires time to reflect. Each event has an objective reality, and an additional "emotional tag" which we attach to it. For example, a traffic jam may occur, causing us to be late for work. That is the objective fact. How we react, though, is up to the emotional tag of significance that we place on it. Do we stay calm, and make plans to finish up a little later? Or, do our emotions cause us to see the traffic as a personal, unfair attack--causing us to seethe and curse? Without the gift of time, we never get to separate emotion from fact. This leads to poor ability to judge the significance of what is happening to us.

In short, then, the ability to modulate behavior comes largely from our pre-frontal lobes, which function primarily as inhibitory centers. Without the luxury of inhibitory brakes, ADHD patients do not get to fully utilize any of their frontal lobe "executive functions."

What are the different kinds of problems in ADHD?

Redefining ADHD as inadequate inhibition explains a wide spectrum of difficulties experienced by people with the syndrome. This expanded spectrum of symptoms can create an environment of havoc. For more details, the reader is referred to the important and inspired works by Barkley, Greene, and Silver listed under Resources.

1. Symptoms of Executive Dysfunction

In the previous section, we defined the components of executive dysfunction. Now, we will translate problems in these areas into real life symptoms.

a. Classical Symptoms of ADHD

ADHD is typically defined as a triad of inattention, impulsivity, and hyperactivity. Figure 2 (see pages 21-22) is a simplified version of the official <u>DSM-IV</u> criteria for ADHD. These are the symptoms that receive the most attention from doctors, and all come from an inability to inhibit.

- *Distractible* <=Inadequate inhibition of extraneous stimuli.

- *Impulsive* <=Inadequate inhibition of internal stimuli.

- *Hyperactive* <=Physically checking out those stimuli.

b. Other Symptoms of Executive Dysfunction

If we do not address the additional resulting executive function issues, we are only dealing with a small part of the problem. These are not just "incidental" symptoms. They are hard to live with—ask either the patient or his family.

- *Lack of foresight!!!* ("Johnny, you'll never get into a good college if you all you do is play videogames. Why do you keep shooting yourself in the foot?") Foresight--the ability to predict the results of our behaviors--is a major adaptive ability of humans. We can run imaginary simulations of the future on our brain's computer. Lack of use of this ability can be the most devastating part of ADHD. Mothers--often endowed with great foresight--are crushed as they watch their child repeatedly head down counter-productive paths.

- *Poor hindsight/Trouble learning from mistakes* ("Johnny, how many times do you have to be punished for the same thing.") Unable to inhibit the present, Johnny cannot stop to consider lessons from the past.

- *Live at the "mercy of the moment."* ("**Johnny is always swept away by whatever is happening to him right then and there.**") **ADHD behaviors make sense once we realize that they are based on reactions taking only the present moment into account. It is not that Johnny doesn't** *care* **about the future; it is that the future and the past don't even exist. Such is the nature of the disability. By way of analogy, imagine riding down a river with a leaking canoe. You would be so overwhelmed by the need to bail out water that you would not see the upcoming cliff. It's not that you don't "care" about falling over a cliff--it's that you don't even get to consider it. If you want to understand the ADHDer's actions, simply ask yourself: "What behavior makes sense if you feel like you only have 4 seconds left to live?"**

- *Poor organization* ("Johnny, you never told me that there is a paper due tomorrow! And, "Why do I have to keep going back to school for your books?" And, "Why didn't you hand in your homework?")

- *Trouble returning to task* ("Johnny, you never complete anything. You get distracted and don't bother finishing. You just don't care.")

- *Poor sense of time* ("Johnny, what have you been doing all afternoon? You can't spend one hour on the first paragraph!")

- *Time moves too slowly* ("Mommy, you are taking forever to go shopping!")

- *Poor ability to utilize "self-talk"* to work through a problem ("Johnny, what were you thinking?! Did you ever think this through?")

- *Poor sense of self awareness* (Johnny's true answer to the above question is probably "I don't have a clue. I guess I wasn't actually thinking.")

- *Poor internalization and generalization of rules* ("Johnny, why do I need to keep reminding you that playing videogames comes *after* you finish your homework?")

- *Poor reading of social clues* ("Johnny, you're such a social klutz. Can't you see that the other children think that's weird?")

- *Inconsistent work and behavior.* ("Johnny, if you could do it well yesterday, why is today so horrible.) With 100% of their energy, they may be able to control the task that most of us can do with 50% of our focus. But who can continually muster 100% effort? As the joke goes: ADHD children do something right once, and we hold it against them for the rest of their lives.

- *Trouble with transitions* ("Johnny, why do you curse at me when I'm just calling you for dinner?")

- *Hyper-focused at times* ("When Johnny is on the computer, I can't get him off. And once his father gets his mind on something, off he goes!")

- *Poor frustration tolerance* ("Johnny, why can't you even let me help you get over this?")

- *Frequently overwhelmed* ("Mommy, just stop. I can't stand it. Just stop. Please!")

- *Gets angry frequently and quickly* ("Johnny, you get flooded with emotion so quickly. Why are you always angry with me? Even though you usually apologize, it still hurts me.")

- *Push away those whose help they need the most* ("Mommy, stop checking my assignment pad. Get out!").

- *"Hyper-responsiveness"* ("Mommy, you know I hate sprinkles on my donuts! You never do anything for me! I hate you!") Barkley uses the term hyper-responsiveness to indicate that people with ADHD have excessive emotions. Their responses, however, are appropriate to what they are actually feeling. So next time you see someone "over-reacting," realize that they are actually "over-feeling," and must feel really awful at that moment.

- *Inflexible/explosive reactions* ("Johnny, you're stuck on this. No, I can't just leave you alone. Johnny, now you're incoherent. Johnny, just stay away. I can't stand it when you break things!") Greene (see Resources) goes into extensive explanation about the inflexible/explosive child.

- *Feels calm only when in motion* ("He always seems happiest when he is busy. Is that why he stays at work so late?")

- *Thrill seeking behavior* ("He seems to crave stimulation at any cost. In fact, he feels most 'on top of his game' during an emergency.")

- *Trouble paying attention to others* ("My husband never listens when I talk to him. He just cannot tolerate sitting around with me and the kids. He doesn't "pay attention" to his family any more than he "paid attention" in school.") As the patient gets older, people in his life will increasingly expect more time and empathy to be directed their way. Yet, the behaviors above of ADHDers may interfere with their demonstration of these traits, despite their passions.

- *Trouble with mutual exchange of favors with friends.* Without establishing a reliable "bank account" of kept promises, friendships can be hard to make.

- *Sense of failure to achieve goals* ("Somehow, I never accomplished all that I thought I could or should have.") This deep disappointment is commonly what brings adults with ADHD to seek help.

- *Lying, cursing, stealing, and blaming others* become frequent components of ADHD; especially as the child gets older. According to some particularly depressing data by Russell Barkley, here is how ADHD children compare to typical children:

Symptom	ADHD Children (%)	Typical Children (%)
Argues with adults	72	21
Blames others for own mistakes	66	17
Acts touchy or easily annoyed	71	20
Swears	40	6
Lies	49	5
Stealing (not involving threats)	50	7

[Barkley RA, Fischer M, et al. The Adolescent outcome: An 8-year prospective follow up. Journal of the American Academy of Child and Adolescent Psychiatry, 29, 546-557.]

- In short, the symptoms of ADHD become less "cute" as the children switch from elementary to secondary schools. The "good" news comes from understanding that these problems are commonly part of the syndrome we call ADHD. They are nobody's fault--not yours, and not your child's. This understanding points the way towards coping with these issues.

2. Co-Occurring Disorders Associated with ADHD

In addition to the executive dysfunctions above, there are a myriad of co-occurring disorders that frequently accompany the diagnosis of ADHD in the patient and/or her family. These disorders may often be *misdiagnosed as* ADHD, or they may *co-exist with* true ADHD. In addition, many people are "subsyndromal," and have just parts of the following diagnosis. John Ratey (see Resources) refers to these as "shadow syndromes." The presence of these disorders must be investigated whenever the diagnosis of ADHD is being considered.

[Medications for the co-occurring disorders in children are used frequently "off-label," and information is quite limited. Recommendations need to be taken as subject to change and debate. Full discussion of the usefulness, monitoring, drug interactions, etc. of these medications is beyond this book. The reader is referred to <u>ADHD with Comorbid Disorders</u> by Pliszka (see Resources), which forms much of the basis for the following medication assessments. Medical treatment of the associated disorders is perhaps best done in consultation with a neurologist or psychiatrist.]

a. Learning Disabilities (LD)

Twenty to thirty percent of patients with ADHD have LD. A review of the diagnostic criteria for ADHD (see Figure 2 on pages 21-22) will show that an Organizational Disability is virtually built into the syndrome of ADHD by definition. Following directions, sequencing problems and dysgraphia are also particularly common. Learning disabilities should be suspected whenever a student does not "live up to his/her potential." They are identified with history, exam and psycho-educational testing. As well explained by Larry Silver (see Resources), learning disabilities can either exacerbate or mimic ADHD. After all, how long can someone focus on something that she does not understand?

b. Disruptive Behavioral Disorders

50% of ADHD children have Disruptive Behavioral Disorders. Even in the absence of a full diagnosis, the lives of many (if not most) children with ADHD are afflicted by lying, cursing, taking things that do not belong to them, blaming others, and being easily angered. This frequency is not surprising given the executive dysfunction hypothesis. Full definitions can be found in the Diagnostic and Statistical Manual-IV. Medications such as mood stabilizers (eg. Depakote), Catapres, and Risperdal can sometimes help with impulsivity and aggression.

- Oppositional Defiant Disorder (ODD). Whereas ADHD children do not comply because of inattention or impulsivity, ODD children are unwilling to conform (even with an intriguing task). They may be negative, deliberately annoying or argumentative, angry and spiteful.

- Conduct Disorder (CD). Children with CD are more frequently overtly hostile and law breaking, with lack of remorse, not seen in ADHD alone. These people violate the rights of others, such as with physical cruelty to others or animals, stealing, etc.

- Antisocial Personality Disorder. People with Antisocial Personality Disorder have a pervasive pattern of severe violation of the rights of others, typically severe enough to merit arrest.

c. Anxiety Disorder

Anxiety Disorder occurs in up to 30% of children with ADHD, but half of the children never tell their parents! Patients are beset most days by painful worries not due to any imminent stressor. Children may appear edgy, stressed out, tense, or sleepless. There may be panic attacks or an incomplete (or negative) response to stimulants.

Treatments include:

- Change of environment; behavioral approaches; exercise; meditation.

- Selective Serotonin Uptake Inhibitors (SSRIs) such as Luvox, Paxil, Prozac, and Zoloft.

- busplrone (Duspar)   helps anxiety but not panic attacks.

- clonazepam (Klonopin)—helps anxiety.

- Tricyclics—help some with anxiety; great for panic attacks. Cardiac concerns.

- Stimulants may help if anxiety is a secondary problem, but may also worsen anxiety.

d. Obsessive Compulsive Disorder (OCD)

Obsessive thoughts and compulsive actions may occur in up to one third of ADHD patients. If ADHD is living in the present, then OCD is living in the future. Although difficult to live with, the future goal directed behavior of OCD might help overcome the organizational problems of ADHD. SSRI's are the current mainstay of medical treatment.

e. Major Depression

Depression occurs in 10-30% of ADHD children and in 47% of ADHD adults. Although pure ADHD patients get depressed briefly, they flow with the environment (changing within minutes). In contrast, depressed children stay depressed for long periods. The symptoms include loss of joy, sadness, pervasive irritability (not just in response to specific frustrations), withdrawal, self-critical outlook, and vegetative symptoms (abnormal sleep or appetite).

Treatment:

- Counseling; adjusting environment.

- Selective Serotonin Uptake Inhibitors (SSRIs) such as Luvox, Paxil, Prozac, and Zoloft.

- bupropion (Wellbutrin)—helps depression and ADHD.

15

- venlafaxine (Effexor)—helps depression and maybe ADHD.

- Tricyclics (such as Tofranil and Pamelor) do not appear to work in children for depression in controlled clinical trials.

f. Bipolar Depression

Bipolar depression occurs in up to 20% of ADHD children. These children show depression cycling with abnormally elevated, expansive, grandiose, and pressured moods. Children may cycle within hours. Other hallmarks include severe separation anxiety and often precociousness as children; extreme irritability; extreme rages that last for hours; very goal directed behavior; and little sleep requirement. They may demonstrate hypersexuality; gory dreams; extreme fear of death; extreme sensitivity to stimuli; often oppositional or obsessive traits; heat intolerance; craving for sweets; bedwetting; hallucinations; possible suicidal tendencies or substance abuse. Often symptoms are shown only at home. See The Bipolar Child by Papolos (under Resources)

Consider bipolar when a diagnosis of "ADHD" is accompanied by above symptoms or:

- strong family history of bipolar disorder or substance abuse.

- *prolonged* temper tantrums and mood swings. Sometimes the angry, violent, sadistic, and disorganized outbursts last for hours (vs. less than 30 minutes in ADHD).

- bipolar rages are typically from parental limit setting; in ADHD, rages are from overstimulation.

- oppositional/defiant behaviors.

- explosive and "intentionally" aggressive or risk seeking behavior.

- substance abuse.

- separation anxiety, bad dreams, disturbed sleep; or fascination with gore.

16

- morning irritability which lasts hours (vs. minutes in ADHD).

- symptoms worsen with stimulants.

Medical treatment:

- valproate (Depakote).

- carbamazepine (Tegretol) clearly helps bipolar and aggressive symptoms at least in adults (no controlled studies in children).

- lithium (not clear that it works in children who cycle so rapidly; does not help ADHD).

- Plus cautious use of stimulants or antidepressants for ADHD symptoms.

- Stimulants and antidepressants may trigger mania.

- Plus risperidone (Risperdal) for psychotic symptoms and aggression.

g. Tics and Tourette's (motor & vocal tics)

Seven percent of ADHD children have tics; but 60% of Tourette's patients have ADHD.

Medical treatments include:

- clonidine (Catapres) / guanfacine (Tenex)—help impulsivity & tics.

- stimulants—helps ADHD but may worsen (or improve) tics.

- tricyclics—mild ADHD help but tic "neutral." Cardiac concerns.

h. Asperger's Syndrome

ADHD and Asperger's syndrome can cluster together. Symptoms include impaired
ability to utilize social cues such as body language, irony, or other "subtext" of
communication; restricted eye contact and socialization; limited range of
encyclopedic interests; perseverative, odd behaviors; didactic, monotone voice;
"concrete" thinking; over-sensitivity to certain stimuli; and unusual movements.

See Attwood's book (Resources).

i. Sensory Integration (SI) Dysfunction

SI dysfunction is the inability to process information received through the senses. The
child may be either oversensitive or undersensitive to stimuli. Or, the child may not
be able to execute a coordinated response to the stimuli. SI may mimic or co-exist
with ADHD. SI is typically evaluated by an occupational therapist. See
Kranowitz's book (Resources). Some types of SI include:

- Hypersensitive to touch: sensitive to clothes or getting dirty; withdraw to
light kiss.

- Hyposensitive to touch: wallow in mud; rub against things; unaware of
pain.

- Hypersensitive to movement: avoid running, climbing, or swinging.

- Hyposensitive to movement: rocking; twirling; unusual positions.

- May also respond abnormally to sights, sounds, smells, tastes or textures.

- May be clumsy; have trouble coordinating (bilateral) movements; or have
poor fine motor skills.

3. Familial Issues.

This can be of two categories:

a. Family members with their own neuro-psychiatric problems

Family members may have their own ADHD, OCD, depression, anxiety, etc. In fact, a
child with ADHD has a forty percent chance that one of his parents has ADHD.
Such difficulties affect the family's ability to cope with the ADHD child, and may
need to be addressed independently.

b. Stress--created by the child--cycling back to further challenge the patient.

Children or adults with ADHD can create chaos throughout the entire family, stressing
everyone in the process. The morning routine and homework are frequent (and
lengthy!) sources of dissension. Other siblings are often resentful of the time and
special treatment given to the ADHD child. Mothers, who frequently consider
their child's homework to be their own, find it stressful that "their" homework
never seems to get completed. Fathers come home to discover a family in distress,
and that they are expected to deal not only with a child who is out of control, but
also with the mother who is understandably now losing it, too. Parents may argue
over the "best strategy," a difficult problem since no strategies are even close to
perfect. The unpleasantness of life around someone with ADHD leads to a pattern
of avoidance that only furthers the cycle of anger. *In turn, all of this family turmoil
creates a new source of pressures and problems for the already stressed ADHD
patient to deal with.*

"Will it be okay?" Onward to therapy for ADHD.

In summary, we miss the point when we address only the triad of inattention,
impulsivity, and hyperactivity. These symptoms are only the tip of the iceberg. Much
greater problems have usually been plaguing the family, but often no one has
understood that the associated symptoms described above are part and parcel of the
same neurologically based condition. Without this recognition, families have thought
that their ADHD child also was "incidentally" uncooperative and apparently self-
absorbed. Unless we recognize that these extended symptoms are part of the same
spectrum, parents will not mention them; and doctors will never deal with them.

Given all of this, it is reasonable to ask: "Will this go away?" Personally, I would re-
phrase the question as, "Will it be OK?" The answer can be "yes," but we must
recognize that this is often the "fifty year plan." In other words, these children can be

wonderfully successful adults, while they continue to work on these issues over their lifetime. Meanwhile, we "just" need to patiently steer them in the positive direction. That is what the rest of this book is all about.

Finally, we must also keep in mind that some of the iceberg is fantastic and enviable. While the rest of us are obsessing about the future, or morosing about the past, people with ADHD are experiencing the present. ADHDers can be a lot of fun; dullness is never a problem. Their "Why not?" attitude may free them to take chances that the rest of us may be afraid to take. Their flux of ideas may lead to creative innovations. And most importantly, their extreme passion can be a source of inspiration and accomplishment to the benefit of us all.

It's going to be quite a ride.

Figure 2. Simplified DSM-IV criteria for ADHD

A. Either (1) or (2)

    (1) Six or more symptoms of **inattention**

        (a) fails to give close attention; careless mistakes

        (b) difficulty sustaining attention

        (c) does not seem to listen when spoken to directly

        (h) easily distracted by extraneous stimuli

        (e) difficulty organizing tasks

        (d) fails to follow through (not volitional or incapable)

        (f) avoids tasks requiring sustained organization

        (g) loses things needed for tasks

        (i) often forgetful in daily activities

    (2) Six or more symptoms of **hyperactivity-impulsivity**

        Hyperactivity

        (a) fidgets/squirms

        (b) leaves seat

        (c) runs or climbs excessively

        (d) difficulty playing in leisure activities quietly

        (e) "on the go" or "driven by a motor"

(f) talks excessively

Impulsivity

(a) blurts out answers before questions completed

(b) difficulty waiting turn

(c) interrupts or intrudes

B. Some symptoms present before 7 y.o.

C. Symptoms in two or more settings

D. Interferes with functioning

E. Not exclusively part of other syndrome

[The symptoms of inattention have been grouped together and placed in italics by the author to demonstrate how much disorganization is built into the definition of ADHD.

Using these criteria, DSM-IV defines three subtypes of ADHD:

ADHD, Predominantly Inattentive Type.

ADHD, Predominantly Hyperactive-Impulsive Type.

ADHD, Combined type.

[Note, that by current terminology, your diagnosis will be "ADHD" even if you don't have hyperactivity.]

Behavioral Checklist
© Pediatric Neurological Associates. May copy for patient use.

Child's Name: Your Name:
Date: Subject (if teacher):

Please rate the severity of each problem listed.   **Please add comments**
below!
(0)none   (1)slight   (2)moderate   (3)major

Trouble attending to work that child understands well_____
Trouble attending to work that child understands poorly___
Requires one-to-one attention to get work done _____
Impulsive (trouble waiting turn, blurts out answers)_____
Hyperactive (fidgity, trouble staying seated) _____
Disorganized _____
Homework not handed in _____
Inconsistent work and effort _____
Poor sense of time _____
Does not seem to talk through problems _____
Over-reacts _____
Easily overwhelmed _____
Blows up easily _____
Trouble switching activities _____
Hyper-focused at times _____

Poor handwriting _____
Certain academic tasks seem difficult (specifiy) _____

Seems *deliberately* spiteful, cruel or annoying _____
Anxious, edgy, stressed or painfully worried _____
Obsessive thoughts or fears; perseverative rituals_____
Irritated for hours or days on end (not just frequent, brief blow-ups)_____
Depressed, sad, or unhappy _____
Extensive mood swings _____
Tics: repetitive movements or noises _____
Poor eye contact _____
Does not catch on to social cues _____
Limited range of interests and interactions _____

Unusual sensitivity to sounds, touch, textures, movement or taste_____
Coordination difficulties _____
Other (specify) _____

If the child is on medication, please answer the following questions:
Can you tell when the child is on medication or not?
Does the medication work consistently throughout the day?
Does the child appear to be on too much or too little medication?

Other comments:

Chapter 2

Home Therapy:

Just STOP!

Home Survival Basics:

Swears, Lies, and Videogames

First, the bad news: many kids with ADHD are afflicted by numerous traits that are difficult to deal with. If we want to maximize our child's chance for a successful future--and avoid our own institutionalization--we had better learn some behavioral approaches to ADHD. It is hard to pick out *the* most important piece of advice. Problems and priorities change over time. But if your life is so hectic that you can't even get the time to read this whole chapter, read the section "Just STOP!"

Besides the works of Barkley, Greene, Phelan and others, many of the guidelines below are inspired by Chris A. Zeigler Dendy's book entitled TEENAGERS WITH ADD: A Parent's Guide. (See "Resources.") This excellent book empathically offers many additional practical suggestions for achieving success with ADHD at home and at school.

Maintain a Disability Outlook

The good news is that these problems are nobody's fault. Not your child's; not yours. Indeed, the key to addressing these symptoms is to adopt what Barkley calls a "disability perspective." They are true disabilities, just like problems with their inattention and learning. These symptoms happen to the ADHD person, as much as they happen to the people around them. No one chose to have these problems. Hate ADHD, not the person with it.

There are several reasons why it is hard to accept these undesirable behaviors as "real" disabilities:

- *Unlike blindness or deafness, there is no external marker for these disabilities.* As an example, consider a child who is deaf and has ADHD. No one would ever think of yelling at the child for his hearing problem. That would be blatantly ridiculous and unfair. Yet, when the same child over-reacts or is easily annoyed as part of his ADHD, it is much harder to accept those difficulties as an innate disability.

- *Unlike physical disabilities, these personality problems often get directed at the caregiver.* The deaf child, for example, is having difficulties but is not attacking us. Her problems evoke from us an instinct to aid her. In contrast, the ADHD child may yell or curse at the parent who is merely trying to help. In short, ADHDers are often not acting in an easily lovable way. No wonder that these disabilities are harder to accept.

- *When our child acts up, the rest of society--along with us--tends to think of bad parenting as being the problem.* As the child pulls candy off of the rack at the supermarket checkout line, we are sure everyone else is thinking, "Why can't you control that child? What is wrong with *you!?*"

- *To accept that some people have a physiological reason for difficulty controlling their behavior runs counter to our deep convictions about who we are.* Our society feels that we are under the control of our "personality," or "will," or "soul." It is hard for us to accept that these aspects of ourselves are so heavily under the control of neurotransmitters.

A disability outlook is not as much "fun" as just considering ADHDers as "unique individuals with special traits." However, while we DO need to celebrate their differences as much as possible, the disability outlook helps because:

- It cuts through the issue of "blame," either of the child or the parents.
- It points the way for parents to see themselves as "therapists" for their problematic child--not as victims of him.
- A realistic assessment of your child's starting point helps minimize your anger and frustration with her when she doesn't live up to what you would like.

Keep it positive.

- Celebrate ADHD strengths: the energy, the "why not?" attitude, the ability to live in the present.

- However, given all of the ADHDer's problems, it is sometimes hard to find anything to praise. Find some accomplishment to laud, and some activity to enjoy together. Laugh with each other. Keep a sense of humor. Hug.

- Remember that ADHD kids are typically a few years behind in social development. Adjust your expectations accordingly.

- When she is finally ready to apologize, talk, or cuddle; take her up on her offer right then and there. Your goal is to put some good times into your relationship. Take them as they come.

- Let your child know that you believe in him/her, despite the disabilities.

- When criticism is required, criticize the behavior, not the child.

- Try to avoid punishing bad behavior. Rather, Barkley suggests rewarding the good behavior you would rather replace it with. For example, instead of punishing cursing, reward each day when language remains civil.

- Only positive rewards will change behavior *and* improve attitude.

- When things start going badly, redirect to a positive direction rather than criticizing the misbehavior. For example, if the child is fighting with her sister, then suggest a new activity, rather than hand out a punishment.

- **Don't nag.** It hasn't worked yet. If you don't have anything nice to say, don't say it. Even simple comments like "How was your day?" may cause frustration in your child.

- **Don't lecture.** It doesn't work either. Plus, given their sense of time, ADHDers will find the experience interminable. Instead, give one or two brief, clear instructions. "Insight transplants" from you to your child, as Thomas Phelan calls them, are unlikely to work. (See Phelan's excellent book Surviving Your Adolescents.)

- **Don't argue.** It takes two to fight. No argument can occur without your permission.

- **Don't offer unscheduled, spontaneous "advice."** What are the odds that your Nintendo playing teen will respond pleasantly to your request to discuss right now that book report due in two weeks?

- Phelan calls these last four points "The Four Cardinal Sins." These "sins" are ineffective and actually harmful. Why would we use them? Instead, either a) decide that the issue is aggravating but not significant enough to warrant intervention (i.e., stay quiet); or b) make an appointment with your child to discuss the issue. Other strategies are described below.

If it's not actually useful, don't do it.

An interaction between you and your child can fall into one of three categories: a) useful; b) useless; or c) counter productive. Actually, there is no such thing as the "useless" category. All useless interventions actually fall eventually into counter-productive, because they just lead to further frustration all around—making the next interaction even less likely to be helpful. Sometimes, relationships are at the point when a simple "Hello, how are you?" consistently provokes an irritated response. So, if the question is not useful, don't ask it. If asking the child to clean up his room has not worked for 12 years, it probably won't be effective today. At these times, Phelan suggests that if you don't have anything really nice to say (e.g.: "Here's five bucks just because I feel like it"), then stay quiet.

Amazingly, many of us keep using the same "useless" or harmful strategies over and over again, as if they might magically work on the 401st try. An unproductive chide or ineffective command may make you feel better for two seconds, but won't improve your child's life--or your relationship with her. So why do it? Seriously.

Seek to understand.

- Listen when the child talks. Teach and model the skill of first rephrasing what the other said. Then respond.

- Ask yourself: "Why did he do that?" There *is* a reason, even if it does not appear rational. Often, the behaviors make sense if we remember that ADHD children live almost exclusively in the present without much ability for foresight. For example, they may want to play Nintendo rather than do homework. If we remember that they are living in the present, choosing to play Nintendo right now actually makes sense.

- Don't take it personally. (Easier said than done.) Remember that this is a disability. You just happen to be the person in the room.

Let the teen be a partner.

- Involve the teen in the problem-solving process.

- Try to give choices. This empowers the child.

- Negotiate!!! Teach and model flexibility. Teach seeking win-win solutions. Keep expectations reasonable. The time to negotiate is *before* you take a final stand. Final stands remain final.

- Stickers and token reward systems do not work in secondary school age children. They need to feel more like a partner.

- Younger children may respond to sticker charts or token systems as described under "Plan A" below.

Restore the child's basic desire to please before attempting behavioral systems.

Reward systems rely on children's natural desire to please their parents. If a child's basic relationships with her parents are so full of anger and resentment that she no longer finds pride in pleasing her parents, then those basic relationships need some healing first, before behavioral modification programs are likely to be successful. Set aside a period of special time (up to 30 minutes) where the goal is simply to exist together pleasantly in the same room. The child gets to choose the (reasonable) activity, and the parent gets to enjoy being near their child without provoking a world war. Avoid saying anything critical--even if it *would* be helpful. Keep questions and comments (even positive ones) to a minimal level. After all, interruptions are still annoying. The goal here is to put your account of good/bad interactions into a positive balance, making it more likely for the child to want to please you. That sets the stage for smoother discipline setting in the future. Dr. David Rabiner (see http://www.helpforadd.com/behtreat.htm) and Dr. Russell Barkley (see Resources) provide a full explanation of this technique.

Plan A: Behavior modification using rewards and punishments.

In order for typical behavior modification and reward systems to be used, the following criteria must be met:

- The behavior must be worth the effort of changing.

- The child must have the ability to consistently control the behavior.

- The reward/punishment is likely to work. (For example, punishment is unlikely to correct forgetful behavior.)

- Those with allegedly cooler heads can apply the plan consistently.

- It is the child's problem.

If these criteria are met, consider plans under Reward/Token Systems.

Reward/Token Systems

- Children with ADHD need frequent, strong, and immediate feedback and rewards.

- The rules need to be succinctly reviewed at the scene before they are needed.

- ADHDers are drawn towards the most attractive stimulus. Reward systems capitalize on this trait by using a "carrot" to lead the child in a productive direction.

- "But don't 'bribes' lead them to do things for the wrong reasons?" Yes, but they already haven't responded to the "right" reasons. That appeal has already failed by the time enticements are added.

- The rewards will need frequent rotation to maintain their power.

- When punishment is required, keep it immediate and controlled. You are not really trying to punish; presumably, you are trying to correct future behaviors. A modest, immediate punishment is likely to be at least as effective as a prolonged one. A spiral of increasing punishments is unlikely to work, and just saddles everyone with a prolonged period of unhappiness in the future.

- Enticements can be as simple as "First we work, then we get to play." Or, "If you only tease your sister twice this week, then you get your allowance."

- Formal systems are described in many books, including those by Silver and Barkley (see "Books and links"). Token systems entail earning points for good behavior (or loosing them for bad behavior) that are then traded in for any privilege.

- Practically speaking, formal token systems are difficult to maintain, and work best with elementary school children.

Most typical children will respond well to typical enticements and threats of punishment. If you made it this far, your child probably isn't one of them. You are ready for:

Plan B: Behavior modification via staying calm to prevent "meltdowns."

Escalating threats don't work when the problem is that the ADHDer is already overwhelmed.

Consider the two following scenarios:

First scenario: Mother: "John, can you please go do two hours of homework?"

John: "Stop! Go away!"

Second scenario: Mother: "John, can I make you fresh pancakes for breakfast?"

John: "Stop! Go away!"

What's going on here? John gives the same response whether asked about something good or bad. His negative response clearly has nothing to do with the actual request. It has to do with his being interrupted. It has to do with his being overwhelmed. It has to do with his ADHD. Obviously, rewards and punishments won't work in this setting. The problem is an inability to control a sensation of being overwhelmed, not a problem with motivation. (After all, you are already offering fresh pancakes.)

When typical rewards and punishments don't work, you may need an approach that Ross Greene refers to as "Plan B." Here, our focus is on preventing over-heated meltdowns. We anticipate problems and try to head them off: we stop, we stay calm, and we negotiate if possible.

"Just Stop!" is the key-- for the ADHD person <u>and</u> you.

STOP! Those four letters are the key to behavioral treatment for most people with ADHD. The exclamation point is a reminder of how important the step is; and how hard it can be, as well.

As described so well by Russell Barkley, the primary difficulty in ADHD is a lack of inhibition of the present (so that you can use your other executive functions to plan the future). In other words, people with ADHD have trouble putting on the brakes. They have trouble stopping. Nothing good comes from speeding out of control. So, their first step is to just STOP!

Once everyone stops, then time can cool our minds. The brakes come on. Executive function can regain control. We can chart a productive course.

There are several amazing things that come from just stopping (if you can do it):

1. *It works!* Time heals. Even 5 or 10 minutes is usually enough for even the most ADHD brain to regain composure. If it routinely takes more than 30 minutes to regain it, consider other diagnoses such as depression or bipolar depression.

2. *With the benefit of time to regain composure, most people will reach the right conclusion. They will begin to come around and comply.* If you just state calmly what is expected as you leave the scene of the impending argument, you will be typically surprised that--at some point fairly soon--the child is addressing the situation. Not always. But surprisingly often. After all, ADHDers are usually far from stupid. They <u>know</u> how to think. They <u>know</u> the rules of morality. They <u>know</u>

the right thing to do. They just need a little longer than the rest of us to regain control and sort it all out. A formal procedure for thinking through choices is described in Chapter 5: Cognitive Behavioral Therapy.

3. *Once you and the child have cooled down, the other behavioral methods will usually be quite clear.* In other words, most of the advice in sections on behavioral management will seem almost blatantly obvious--if you are calm. For example, we discuss keeping it positive. We discuss seeking to understand and making the child part of the problem solving process. We discuss choosing only productive punishments. When you are calm, these approaches are not exactly rocket science, and are almost self-evident. When you are screaming, these approaches are not available.

Just Stop. This means you, too.

Yes, you. There is no one else reading this right now. I mean you, the parent. You have to put on the brakes as well. You are a human being who is struggling with self-control also. Although your brain theoretically has normal control, ADHD in the family can be so exacerbating and even demoralizing that our ability to stop and see things clearly is debilitated as well. [Note that there is a forty percent chance that one of the parents also has ADHD--so indeed there may be other reasons why stopping is so hard in these families.]

Why would we expect the child to be the only one trying--and succeeding--at exerting self-control? Why would we expect the only one with a recognized physiological disability in self-control be the only one working on the project? How about ourselves? You may answer, "Well, I'm so overwhelmed and stressed by my environment that it's hard to stay in control." Welcome to the club. That's what your child is experiencing also. You won't let <u>him</u> get away with that excuse....

Not only doesn't it work, screaming at the child is actually counter-productive.

She is already over-whelmed. She is already overloaded and over stimulated. Being screamed at just inflames the situation, and ultimately makes it harder for your child to achieve her goal: regaining composure so that her own brain can reach the right decision.

Warning symptoms of getting overheated

The earliest signs of overload include voices getting raised, muscles tightened, faces reddened, or grunting. This is the time to defuse. At this point, you may be able to salvage the situation with humor, negotiation, redirecting the conversation in a different direction, or maybe even taking a few deep breaths.

A little later, the signs of being overwhelmed get pretty obvious, if we would just listen. They are usually something subtle like: "STOP! Get out! Leave me alone! I can't take it, anymore!" Your child is not making this stuff up. That is how he feels. Pretty awful. Take his advice. Stop. He is actually telling you in clear words just what you need to know: "I need to stop now." Ideally, he would have said it calmly. Ideally.

This is not the time to give in to our impulse to just get it over with. You might have the self-control to do that. Your ADHD child was not born that way. Don't assume that just because you can handle it, that he can as well. All brains have equal rights, but all brains are not constructed the same.

"But what if he doesn't just stop?"

Encourage compliance with the system be ensuring that the child recognizes that this cooling off period is not punishment. It is not like the old punitive "time out" system, which works best with elementary students. Rather, the child gets to go do some pleasant--yet soothing--activity. Consider reading (their choice--magazines and comics are okay), Legos, or listening to music. Adrenaline producing activities such as Nintendo are probably not a good idea. Truly cool activities, like playing on the computer or watching TV may be hard to stop after the intended 5 minutes. Do not forget a similar system for yourself.

If that doesn't work--and there are some oppositional children for whom it won't--then ignore the child. It takes two to fight. No one can enlist you in an argument unless you enter the arena.

After stopping, then state the rule once and leave.

The decision to declare a cooling off period has nothing to do with a decision as to who "won." You are not giving in. Calmly state the rule or action that is required, and end the discussion. Come back later when cool heads prevail.

"But all he ever does is ask to stop. How do we ever get anything done?"

Good point. But, here are your choices:

1. Keep fighting for 30 minutes, get nothing accomplished after that, chip away at your relationship with your child, and increase household frustration levels making the next blowup more likely; or

2. Take a 5-10 minute break, get something accomplished, maintain your relationship with your child, and lower household frustration levels making the next blowup less likely.

When *you* STOP and think about it, the choice is pretty obvious, isn't it? Yet when faced with that choice in the heat of the moment, most of us have been taking the wrong course.

Indeed, this is not always a terribly efficient system. However, neither you nor your child has been dealt great choices. But STOPPING is the least bad option. It certainly beats the alternative of counter-productive screaming. You already know *that* does not work.

Good luck, and do not expect results overnight. This is a multi-year task to learn. Model it well. Once you've stopped, you are ready for the next steps:

After Stopping: Defuse, don't inflame.

*   Your child is already overwhelmed and confused. Parental anger does not work, and only makes the situation worse--but then, you already have discovered that.

*   STAY CALM. That deserves repeating. STAY CALM. (Much easier said than done.)

*   LOWER YOUR VOICE.

*   WALK AWAY. Announce that discussion will begin again once everyone has achieved composure.

- Once calm, negotiate, negotiate, negotiate. Parents need to model negotiation, not inflexibility. Don't worry about losing control: the parent always gets to decide which compromise is accepted.

- PICK YOUR FIGHTS. Is this fight worth chipping away at your relationship with your child? Remember, this is not war. The family that stays <u>together</u> wins.

- ADHD is the inability to inhibit behaviors. Why do we expect ADHDers to be the only ones who actually control themselves? As adults with better self-control, shouldn't we be the first to actually use it?

- Don't say things that you will regret, such as gratuitously hurtful comments or punishments that you cannot enforce.

- For homework, stick calmly by a simple rule: First we work, then we play.

Remember: negative behaviors usually occur because the ADHDer is spinning out of control, not because he is evil. While <u>evil</u> behavior would need to be aggressively squelched, the much more common <u>overwhelmed</u> behavior needs to be calmly defused.

Minimize arguments with the "no-fault" approach

- Zeigler-Dendy has the very useful suggestion that rules be enforced with a no-fault approach. In other words, avoid arguments based on whose fault it is. Just deal with the end results. For example, it doesn't matter why a child arrives home late. It doesn't matter that you forgot to remind her again about the time of her usual curfew. It doesn't matter that the cat ate her watch. It does not matter that the car ran out of gas. It does not matter that you didn't buy her a reliable car. She is late, this is the consequence, and this is the plan to prevent it from happening again. It really simplifies discussion, doesn't it?

- This approach is particularly useful for ADHD people who always blame others for their problems. There is no point in their blaming you if blame is not being made relevant.

- Could this sometimes be unfair? Sometimes, yes. But in the long run, arguments are diminished, and that is to everyone's advantage.

- A second important result of this approach is that it allows us to avoid direct criticism of the child. We punish the end behavior and its end results. We are not directly criticizing the child. After all, we are not assigning blame to anyone. Thus, this approach is a rediscovery of the old adage, "Criticize the behavior, not the child."

Dealing with lying

- Lying is often a part of ADHD. It is part of the disability.

- Lying will typically get better over the long run.

- Lying may occur because the child is totally befuddled how he got into this mess. There simply is no logical explanation (ADHD is not logical), so they make one up.

- Clearly, sticking to a lie once you have been clearly "caught" is not a logical "choice." Observing the unbelievable mental contortions of these children as they muddle through a lie provides a valuable window into their remarkable lack of problem-solving skills.

- Don't set them up to lie. If you already know about an infringement, just state the facts that you know, and proceed with the consequences. Do not use this as an honesty test.

- Minimize the need to lie by eliminating some punishments that the child lies to avoid.

- Develop a plan to solve the original problem area that led to the lie.

Use tangible methods to externalize problem areas.

- Explicitly state out loud the problem and consequences at the time of the event.

- Use timers and planners to break down time into manageable, concrete tasks. Timers will also help keep you from nagging.

- Brainstorm ideas on index cards or word processor. Then, physically sort through and order thoughts.

See also sections on Cognitive Behavioral Therapy, and School Therapy.

Top Principles of ADHD Management

1. Keep a sense of humor. Seek to enjoy, not to scream.

2. Celebrate the ADHD person's humor, creativity, and passion.

3. Hate ADHD, not the person with it.

4. You do not have a standard child. You can view the issue as a disability. Or, you can view it as wonderful uniqueness. Or, you can view it as both. The perspective of "standard," though, is not an option.

5. Recognize that attention issues in the child are only the tip of the iceberg that the whole family must address.

6. The "patient" in ADHD is the whole family.

7. Instead of punishing wrong behavior, set a reward for the correct behavior you would rather replace it with. Rewards should be immediate, frequent, powerful, clearly defined, and consistent.

8. Plan ahead. Give warnings before transitions. Discuss in advance what is expected. Have the child repeat out loud the terms he just agreed to.

9. Don't argue, nag; or attempt unsolicited and spontaneous transplants of your wisdom to your child. Instead, either a) decide that the issue is aggravating but not significant enough to warrant intervention; or b) make an appointment with your child to discuss the issue.

10. Head off big fights *before* they begin. Seek to defuse, not to inflame. When tempers flare, allow everyone to cool off. Serious discussion can only occur during times of composure. **Remember: negative behaviors usually occur because the ADHDer is spinning out of control, not because he is evil. While <u>evil</u> behavior would need to be aggressively squelched, the much more common <u>overwhelmed</u> behavior needs to be calmly defused.**

11. Especially with teens, negotiate, negotiate, negotiate. Parents need to model negotiation, not inflexibility. Don't worry about losing control: the parent always gets to decide when negotiation is over and which compromise is accepted.

12. Pick your fights. Is the issue at hand worth chipping away at your relationship with your child? Can your child really control the offending behavior at this moment?

13. Although it is not the child's "fault," he will still ultimately be the one to take the consequences of his behavior.

14. This is hard work.

15. You will make it through this; you have no choice.

16. "The children who need love the most will always ask for it in the most unloving ways." [Words of a teacher quoted by Russell Barkley.]

17. If it is working, keep doing it. If not, do something else.

18. Forgive your child and yourself nightly. You didn't ask to live with the effects of ADHD any more than did your child.

19. Review this text, and others, periodically. You are going to forget this stuff, and different principles will likely be needed at different stages. A good way to remember to review is by subscription to some of the free monthly newsletters on ADHD (see resources).

20. Steven Covey (<u>The Seven Habits of Highly Effective People</u>) suggests imagining your child delivering your eulogy. What do you want him to say about you? Keep those bigger goals in mind as you choose your interactions/reactions to your child.

21. This is not a contest with your child. The winner is not the one with more points. The winner is the one whose child still loves them when they graduate from high school.

It will most likely turn out O.K.

Remember, the chances for success are good, especially for children with: higher socio-economic status, higher intelligence, better early peer relations, less aggression, less psychopathology in the parents, and less conflict with their parents. We can't solve all of the problems at once. Stay calm. She'll probably get into college even if today's English homework is late. Take one day at a time; this is the 50-year plan. Forgive yourself daily for your own imperfections as you deal with a difficult situation. Have some fun. And keep your endpoint in mind. Your endpoint is not just your child's academic and social success--it also includes a good relationship with you.

Chapter 3

School Therapy:

What Can the School Do?

Martin L. Kutscher, M.D.
Assistant Clinical Professor of Pediatrics and Neurology,
New York Medical College, Valhalla, N.Y.
Pediatric Neurological Associates, White Plains, N.Y.

©2002

Common Sense ADHD School Accommodations

Martin L. Kutscher, M.D.

Any teacher can institute the following suggestions, even without formal student classification:

- *Learn about ADHD.* Typically, teachers in the higher grades have a harder time "believing" in the condition. The older students no longer appear physically hyperactive. Organization and planning problems are frequently misinterpreted as lack of preparation and motivation. The school special education staff should have materials for classroom teachers.

- *Don't take the ADHD behaviors as personal challenges.* The answer to the question "Why can't he listen to me like all of the other children?" is that he can't turn off his ADHD at will. It isn't personal.

- *Take a realistic outlook at the child you get every day.* Periodically, rate the ADHD behaviors using Dr. Phelan's brief checklist (1 means very little; 10 means a lot)

  - Inattentiveness _____
  - Impulsivity _____
  - Difficulty delaying gratification _____
  - Emotional overarousal _____
  - Hyperactivity _____
  - Non compliance _____
  - Social problems _____
  - Disorganization _____

  This is your starting point. Not a typical child. This is what you can likely expect from him every day. Once teachers and parents accept this starting point (which I assure you the child does not exactly want, either), it is easier not to take everything so personally. Also, anger on the caregiver's part is reduced--since anger arises when there is greater discrepancy between what you expected versus what you got. The parents can also fill out the checklist, and discuss it with the teacher. They will realize that they are allies.

- *Provide help for deficits at the moment it is needed*, not negative feedback when it is already too late. Unfortunately, the simple reality is that punishment does not usually teach the needed behaviors to ADHD kids. This is because many children with ADHD have difficulty "doing what they know," not "knowing what to do." They already "know," for example, that they should come to class prepared. Once we understand that punishment has not been working, we are ready to provide relief for their disabilities by guiding them at the moment guidance is needed— rather than continued disbelief that they did it wrong again.

- Presenting Material to ADHD Children

    - *Have child sit in the front of the class.*

    - *Establish good eye contact.*

    - *Tap on the desk (or use other code) to bring the child back into focus.*

    - *Alert child's attention with phrases such as "This is important."*

    - *Break down longer directions into simpler chunks.*

    - *Check for comprehension.*

    - *Encourage students to underline the key words of directions.*

    - *Encourage students to mark incorrect multiple-choice answers with an "x" first. This allows them to "get started" quickly, while forcing them to read all of the choices before making a final selection.*

    - *Allow physically hyperactive children out of their seats to hand out and pick up papers, etc.*

- Organizational Help

    - *Recognize that disorganization is a major disability for almost everyone with ADHD.* In fact, it is difficult to diagnose ADHD in the absence of organizational problems. Yes, ADHD students can--and frequently do--write a wonderful paper and then forget to hand it in. This striking unevenness in skills is what makes it a learning disability.

- *Ensure that <u>parents</u> and <u>child</u> all know the correct assignment.* Yes, <u>most</u> students can take this responsibility upon themselves. Those with ADHD, though, usually <u>cannot</u>. It is unfair and counter-productive to let intelligent students flounder because of this disability. Once informed of the needed work, the child is still responsible to work (with his/her parents) to get it done. The following options can be used. This part will take work, especially to keep the system going:

  - *Inform about typical routines* (such as quizzes every Friday).

  - *Hand out written assignments for the week; or,*

  - *Initial student's homework assignment pads after each period.* <u>Please</u> do not expect the student to come up after class for the signature on their own. If they were organized enough to do that, we would not need to be doing this. And, yes, the typical student is organized enough to come to the teacher; but this is not the typical student.

  - If unable to initial all new assignments, then be sure to address any occasionally missed work, as below.

- **Notify family immediately of any late assignments** *by one of following.* Waiting for mid-term notices is too late to correct the problem, and too late for the student to behaviorally notice the connection between his/her performance and the consequences. THIS IS KEY!

  - ***A phone call or e-mail* takes the child out of the loop, and works best.**

  - *The parent could call the team leader/guidance counselor each week* for an update.

- *The parent could mail weekly a card to each teacher*. The card would simply have spaces for missed work and comments, and is dropped back into the mail.

- *Allow for expedient make up of late or incorrectly done homework. Late work is expected one day from parental notification.* If deduction for lateness actually works to correct the problem, then keep doing it; if not, recognize the problem as a currently uncorrectable disability. In such a case, the work does need to be completed, but is not fair for a persistent organizational disability to cause excessive and demoralizing deductions. With this notification support, the student does all of the work (i.e., "gets away with nothing") and gets good grades. Without this support, the child "gets away with not doing the work," and gets bad grades.

- If, for some reason, it is necessary to give an "F" for incomplete work, remember that an F is 65, not 0. Trying to get a decent quarterly grade while averaging in a "0" or two is virtually impossible. A grade of "0" is excessive and counter-productive.

- Simple accommodations for other frequently associated problems

    - Dysgraphia (hand writing problems)

        - *Use of a computer.*

        - *Graph paper helps line up math problems.*

        - *Provide a copy of class notes, or arrange for peer to make carbon copy.*

        - *Minimize deductions for neatness and spelling. Instead, give extra points for neatness.*

    - Dyscalculia (math problems)

        - *Liberal use of a calculator, or do every other problem if homework takes too long.*

"Section 504" Accommodations

- Section 504 of the Vocational Rehabilitation Act (Public Law 93-112) is a Federal <u>civil rights</u> law which aims at eliminating discrimination in any program that receives federal funds (including most all US schools and colleges).

- By 504 definition, the disability:

  - can be physical or mental;

  - must substantially limit one or more "life activities" such as *learning*, performing manual tasks, caring for oneself, speaking, hearing, or walking.

- Parents or the school may initiate a 504 evaluation.

- Classification under Section 504 will typically require a school meeting, but less formal psychological and educational testing than classification under IDEA (see below.)

- A written plan for 504 accommodations is not mandated, but certainly makes sense. It should be periodically revised (yearly)

- 504 "accommodations" may be "easier" to obtain as they generally mandate accommodations more than costly special services.

- Accommodations like those listed above under "common sense" can be mandated via Federal Law Section 504 if needed.

- Untimed tests, including SATs, may require 504 classification.

IDEA Classification

- The Individuals with Disabilities Act (IDEA, Part B) of 1990 provides federal funding to schools that guarantee special needs students with appropriate rights and services, including:

- A free appropriate public education. If unable to provide an "appropriate" public education, the school must pay for alternate education.

- IDEA classifiable conditions include:

    - Specific Learning Disability (LD),

    - Emotional and Behavioral Disorder (ED)

    - Other Health Impaired (OHI)

        - The US DOE (Dept. of Education) memo of 1991 includes ADHD as a classifying condition under OHI.

- Parents must be full partners in the process of developing an Individualized Education Plan (IEP). If nothing else, parents certainly know what has not worked so far.

- The school has the right to decide what evaluation is needed.

- The parents may request an independent evaluation if they disagree with the school's evaluation.

- IDEA classification evaluations and provided services are usually more comprehensive than 504 plans.

- Detailed information can be found through the National Information Center for Children and Youth with Disabilities at www.nichcy.org.

- There is annual updating of the IEP, with full re-evaluation every three years. The parents may request review and revision of the IEP at any time.

Chapter 4

Medication Therapy

Martin L. Kutscher, M.D. and Robert Wolff, MD
Departments of Pediatrics and Neurology,
New York Medical College, Valhalla, N.Y.
Pediatric Neurological Associates, White Plains, N.Y.

Disclaimer: This information is presented as an introductory educational resource and is subject to change. It does not constitute medical advice; nor is it a substitute for discussion between patients and their doctors.

Medical Treatment

Ritalin and Related Stimulant Medications

What are stimulant medications?

Ritalin (methylphenidate); Concerta, Metadate CD, Ritalin LA (long lasting forms of methylphenidate), Focalin (just the active part of methylphenidate); Dexedrine (dextroamphetamine); Adderall (a mixture of amphetamines); AdderallXR (long lasting form of Adderall) and Cylert (pemoline) are sometimes called "stimulants". When prescribed for people who have ADHD, they stimulate the frontal parts of the brain that are not inhibiting ("filtering out") distractions as well as they should. The medications work similarly to caffeine. They are not tranquilizers or sedatives. The children appear "calmer" because they are more focused, not because they are sedated. Many children require medication in order to give them the basic tools needed to work on behavioral modifications.

How can these medicines help?

They can improve attention span, decrease distractibility, increase ability to finish tasks, improve ability to follow directions, decrease hyperactivity, and improve ability to think before acting (decrease impulsivity).

Legibility of handwriting and completion of schoolwork and homework can improve. Aggression and stubbornness may decrease in youngsters with ADHD.

Stimulant medication is not the only answer for ADHD! The medicine often works best when used together with special help in school and behavior modification procedures at home and school. Some youngsters and families also benefit from individual, family, or group psychotherapy. If stimulant medications do not help, or cause side effects that are a problem, you can discuss other medications with the doctor.

Should the medicine be taken for homework and weekends?

The quick answer is: take the medication whenever it would lead to the next few hours being a more positive experience for the child. Certainly, this would usually include school hours. However, homework time usually benefits from medication as well, even though many parents try to "tough it out" at home without the medication. Unfortunately, this "martyr" approach--while lovingly intended--is often a mistake for both the child and the parents. It leads to lengthy and excessive yelling sessions during homework, and wears away at family enjoyment of their time together. Isn't your child's relationship with you and the rest of her family as important as her school grades? Use of the longer lasting preparations may help eliminate the need not only for the lunchtime dose, but also for a third dose after school.

How long does the medicine last?

Ritalin, Focalin, and Dexedrine last 3 - 4 hours. Regular Adderall lasts about 4-5 hours. Ritalin SR, Dexedrine Spansules, and Cylert may last at least 6 - 8 hours. Concerta, Metadate CD, and Ritalin LA are long lasting (once daily) forms of methylphenidate which should last 10+ hours. Adderall XR is a long lasting form of Adderall, which also lasts about 10+ hours.

How will the doctor monitor this medicine?

From time to time, the physician (or nurse) will check height, weight, pulse, and blood pressure. When Cylert is used, blood is taken to check on the liver function and blood count -- usually before starting the medicine, and occasionally afterward. The doctor will ask for regular reports from your child's teacher(s) to check on learning and behavior.

What side effects can this medicine have?

Any medication may have side effects, including allergy to the medication. Because each patient is different, your doctor will work with you to get the most positive effects and the fewest negative effects from the medication. The list below may not include rare or unusual side effects. It is important to note that except for a fraction of the children who experience mild appetite or sleep problems, the vast majority of people have no significant side effects from stimulants.

Lack of appetite (Handle by encouraging a good breakfast, and afternoon and evening snacks; give medicine after meals, rather than before. Problem usually resolves.)

Trouble falling asleep, which usually improves over several weeks.

Headaches

Stomachaches

Irritability, crankiness, crying, or emotional sensitivity.

Rapid pulse or increased blood pressure.

Sometimes, as the medicine wears off, hyperactivity or bad moods get worse than before the medicine was started. This is called "rebound". The doctor can make dosage adjustments to help this problem.

A few children may not grow quite as fast as usual. Current research suggests that the culprit is ADHD itself, not the medications used to treat it.

Occasionally, nervous habits (like picking at skin) or stuttering may appear.

Muscle tics or twitches, jerking movements, or vocal noises. It is not clear that these tics can ever be permanantly induced.

Please talk to the doctor if you suspect the medicine is causing a problem.

What could happen if this medicine is stopped suddenly?

There are no medical problems in doing this. A few youths may experience irritability, trouble sleeping, or increased hyperactivity for a day or two, if they have been on daily medication for a long time, especially at above average doses. Occasionally, it is better to stop the medication gradually, over a week or so.

How long will this medicine be needed?

There is no way to know how long a person will need to take the medicine. The parent, the doctor, and the school will work together to find out what is right for each young person. Sometimes the medicine is needed for only a few years, but some people may need help from medicine even as adults.

What else should I know about this medicine?

- Many people have incorrect information about this medicine. If you hear anything that worries you, please check with the doctor.
- This medicine does not cause illegal drug use or addiction. In fact, multiple studies show that use of stimulants in ADHD children greatly REDUCES the risk of future substance abuse (when compared to ADHD children who are not treated). Presumably, those kids whose life is filled with success do not need to turn to alternate forms of seeking pleasure.
- This medicine does not stop working at puberty.
- Some young people take the medicine three or four times a day, every day. Others only need to take it twice a day or once a day on school days. Your doctor and you will work out what is best.
- If a dose is missed, just pick up with the regular dose at the next scheduled time. Do not double up the next dose.
- It is important not to chew long lasting preparations, because this releases too much medicine all at once.
- If the medicine seems to stop working, it may be because it is not being given regularly (especially at school), because your child has gained weight and needs a higher dose, or because something at school or at

home, or in the neighborhood, is upsetting your child Please discuss your concerns with the doctor.

Other Medications for ADHD

In addition to the stimulant medications, there are several other medicines that may also be extremely useful. As anxiety and depression may be very frequent components of Attention Deficit Disorder, it is important to recognize that medicines with an anti-anxiety or anti-depressant effect may prove to be of significant help. The following medications are considered for such therapies:

Strattera (atomoxetine)

Strattera is a recently FDA approved medication for the treatment of ADHD. It selectively increases norepinephrine levels in multiple brain areas, and dopamine levels only in the frontal lobes. As such, it is more "selective" than the "stimulants." Preliminary data suggest that it may not increase tics, insomnia, or anxiety in ADHD patients; and that it may have a role in improving family interactions over a 24-hour period. While initial data look promising, more direct comparisons with the stimulants and more long term follow up will be needed.

Catapres (clonidine) and guanfacine (Tenex)

Catapres and Tenex are "alpha agonists" which have been been chiefly used in the treatment of hypertension in adults. They have been of some use in youngsters with attention deficit problems, particularly for the symptoms of impulsivity. They have been also used to some degree in the treatment of youngsters with tic disorders, such as in Tourette's syndrome. These medications have a potential sedating effect and are probably best given at bedtime initially. Catapres is sometimes used in youngsters who have insomnia to allow them to go to sleep at night at a more reasonable hour. Headaches, dizziness and fatigue are occasional problems with the use of these medications, and need to be monitored carefully. Blood pressure needs to be periodically followed, but rarely becomes a significant problem. Sudden changes in the regimen can cause blood pressure swings, and should be avoided. These medications need to be taken seven days a week.

Tofranil (imipramine)

This "tricyclic antidepressent" is sometimes used as an adjunct to the treatment of ADHD. It provides an anti-anxiety effect without sedation, as well as some improvement of inattention.

When given before bedtime, it may allow the youngster to fall asleep more readily.

In many children, when a stimulant medication is used, they become more focused on their sense of anxiety regarding school performance, social performance, etc. There are many occasions when starting him/her on treatment with Tofranil or a similar agent may be useful even before initiating a trial of stimulant medicine such as Ritalin.

Tofranil has been used for many years by pediatricians in the treatment of simple bed-wetting. In this regard, it has a long safety record. All medicines, of course, have side effects, and Tofranil has its own special list. Perhaps the greatest concern is the small possibility of a potential adverse effect on the cardiac or heart conduction systems. An EKG may be monitored. More commonly, the higher dosages are not at all required in the treatment of mild anxiety. Additionally, there are very rare case reports of liver and bone marrow toxicity. If a youngster is maintained on medication for any length of time, routine blood work to check these functions and drug levels may be performed. Occasionally, constipation, dryness of mouth, blurry vision, fatigue and rapid heartbeat may occur.

Unlike stimulant medication, Tofranil does not work immediately, but often takes close to two weeks before there is any perceived benefit. The most likely benefit is an improved ability to tolerate frustration. The youngster may appear to be more outgoing and sociable as well.

Tofranil is itself a member of a medication group known as the tricyclics. In much higher dosages, these medications are used as anti-depressants. In low dosages, Tofranil and similar agents have been used in the treatment of anxiety attacks.

The mechanism of action of Tofranil is felt related to a decrease in the uptake of norepinephrine at the nerve cell membrane. This pharmacological effect is also similar to that seen with the use of Ritalin.

Elavil (amitriptyline)

Elavil is very similar in its chemical composition to the above-mentioned Tofranil. Elavil is also widely used in the treatment of migraine headaches. Elavil has a tendency to cause a much greater sedation than Tofranil, and is particularly useful in youngsters who have a significant sleep problem. It is given usually an hour before bedtime. Similar to Tofranil, it usually takes a few weeks to show benefits, which include lessened anxiety and a greater threshold for frustration. Its spectrum of side effects is very similar to that of Tofranil. When given in high dosages, it is used also as an anti-depressant medicine.

Prozac (fluoxetine), Paxil, Luvox, Zoloft, Celexa

The Selective Serotonin Re-uptake Inhibitors (SSRIs) such as Prozac are increasingly used in the treatment of depression, obsessive-compulsive disorder and anxiety. It may conceivably have some beneficial effect in ADHD, but most evidence at present is anecdotal. Its increased use by physicians reflects its relative effectiveness as well as safety. Biochemically, it acts as a serotonin uptake blocker. Some of these medications come as both a tablet and a liquid.

During its initiation, it may paradoxically cause a slight increased degree of nervousness or disinhibition. It may also cause some decreased appetite or headache. The medication requires a long time to show effectiveness – anywhere from six to eight weeks. Weight gain and loss of sexual interest are the most common side effects.

Wellbutrin (bupropion)

Wellbutrin is considered a "novel antidepressant" with dopamine agonist and noradrenergic effects. It may improve aggression and hyperactivity, as well as cognition and inattention. It is quite helpful for depression and anxiety, but has no effect on obsessive/compulsive behavior. Although usually well tolerated, it may rarely precipitate tics or seizures.

Risperdal (risperidone)

Risperdal is an "atypical neuroleptic" that is quite effective in the treatment of tic disorders and explosive behaviors. Its role in the treatment of inattention is debated. Side effects include possible weight gain, sedation, and rarely a serious reaction called malignant hyperthermia. The risk of a permanent movement disorder (called tardive dyskinesia) related to its long-term use is probably quite low.

Effexor (venlafaxine)

This medication has noradrenergic and serotinergic properties. Limited studies in adults suggest effectiveness in ADHD.

Medication for Co-Occurring Disorders

Medication treatment for the co-occurring disorders associated with ADHD are discussed in Chapter 1.

Selected Web site

Internet Mental Health (www.mentalhealth.com) has an excellent pharmacy section.

Chapter 5

Cognitive Behavioral Therapy:

Talking Ourselves Through a Problem

Talking Ourselves Through a Problem: Cognitive Behavioral Therapy

Introduction

> *Mother: "Johnny, please get up. It's time for school. If you don't start now, you won't have time for a nice, hot breakfast; and I won't be able to drive you to the bus."*
>
> *Johnny: "No. Go away. Leave me alone!"*

Poor way to respond, isn't it? Day after day, it's hard to fathom how Johnny could choose this ineffective response. But that is just the point. Johnny isn't choosing anything. In fact, he isn't even thinking. He's just reacting. This is because people with ADHD do not inhibit their reactions long enough to talk themselves through the problem.

Typically, people with ADHD have difficulty with "self-talk," i.e., using words to think through a situation. In addition, they make poor choices because they have trouble inhibiting their behavior. If given the correct words with which to calmly consider the problem, they typically know the correct answer. As Russell Barkley points out, ADHD children have a deficiency doing what they know, not in knowing what to do. (See the concept of executive dysfunction in ADHD in Chapter 1.)

If people actually stopped to listen to themselves working through the above situation, this is what they would hear:

What's the problem?
- I have to get up even though I don't want to.

What are my possible solutions?
- I could rant and rave, scream miserably, get punished, lose all of my privileges, and end up going to school anyway--like always.

- I could get up, have a reasonably pleasant breakfast, be praised for being so helpful, and go to school.

What choice will I make?
- Well, when you put it that way, it is not really that tough a choice, is it? I end up going to school either way. But, the first way I get punished; and the second way, I get rewarded. How stupid do you think I am? Of course, it makes sense to just get up calmly.

How did I do?
- Pretty well, don't you think? Why didn't I ever think of it this way before? I guess because I never actually *thought* about it before, at least not with words.

What we all need to do when faced with a problem (but ADHD children never learned to do automatically) is to use our brain's computer to analyze the problem and choose the most effective response. Sometimes, the most productive response is not the most emotionally enticing. In these cases, we depend on the thinking part of our brain to exercise "cognitive override." As helpers to people with ADHD, then, we must help their cognitive abilities override their impulsive emotions--by utilizing the skill of self-talk. This process is called "Cognitive Behavioral Therapy."

General Concepts of Cognitive Behavioral Therapy

- The following technique is adapted from Philip C. Kendall and Lauren Braswell's book Cognitive Behavioral Therapy for Impulsive Children by Guilford Press.
- "Cognitive" refers to using the thinking—and particularly verbal—parts of our brain to control our actions. Speech is the tool by which humans formulate and manipulate complex ideas.
- "Behavioral" refers to the use of rewards to encouraging use of the technique.

- These skills require practice when the child is calm. Don't try them initially during stressful times. This is one of the times when you must "strike while the iron is cold."

- These techniques are best taught by a professional therapist.

- We should model the process frequently. We need to demonstrate flexibility, and we need to demonstrate it verbally.

- Time moves very slowly for children with ADHD. At first, the process will seem unnecessary and interminable to them. Be patient.

- This will not work overnight. We are talking about years, if not a lifetime, for ADHD people to master these skills. But what other choice do we have?

- Many ADHD children will not be ready to fully employ these techniques until they have become sufficiently miserable with what they have done to their lives. Hopefully, we can pre-empt that time; or, at least, have the person prepared with the skills for when he *is* finally motivated to use them.

- Parents and teachers could use a little cognitive therapy on themselves, as well. When we wake our child up in the morning, what is our goal? Is it to facilitate a pleasant experience for everyone and have our child like being around us, or is it to prove that we can force him to make his bed?

- NEGOTIATION will be a large part of the successful answers. We are seeking to teach our children how to achieve win-win solutions. Sometimes these solutions will be less then we would ideally like. More likely, they will be just fine compromises, as long as we can get over any negative connotation to the word "compromise." Don't worry. You are still in control. You still get to choose when to compromise (virtually always except for safety issues) and what the final terms of the compromise will be. The process certainly beats the alternative: enduring meltdowns or the whittling down of our relationships with our child.

- The following 5 steps need to be explained to the child, and then the child should put each step into his/her own words.

Five Steps of Cognitive Behavioral Therapy

(1) Stop!

- There's that need to just STOP again.
- This step is initially the hardest.
- We can't exercise our powers of self-talk and reason while our brain is being overwhelmed by emotion. This applies to people with or without ADHD.
- Ideally, both the parent and child learn to sense impending emotional overload before it happens.
- The best way to treat a meltdown is to prevent it. Learn the warning signs. Often, they are not very subtle. For example, the child might scream. "Stop, I can't take it anymore."
- Often, just the act of saying "Stop," and taking a deep breath will be enough of a break.
- Other times, a formal disengagement will be required. Agree, in advance, to a system whereby the child can have a safe, non-punitive place to calm down when needed. The calming down activity should basically be whatever the child wants. Remember, pulling back from the brink is difficult. We are trying to increase the chances that the child will comply.
- Once a meltdown occurs, it typically must run its course before rational discussion can be expected.
- Once a state of calm is present, we can proceed to the actual process.

(2) What is the problem?

- Formulate, in words, "what is the problem we are trying to solve?" What are the goals?
- In order to better understand the problem, "seek first to understand." Where is the other person coming from? What are his/her needs? Why would they possibly be acting this way?

- As a practical step, start formulating the problem by re-stating out loud what the other person just said. This step will force us to listen to what has just been said to us, and will reassure the speaker that we are indeed listening to them.
- Without the language of self-talk, many ADHDers find themselves overwhelmed without coherent thoughts. How do we know when that is happening? Simple. The child starts screaming.
- Examples of formulating the problem:
  o "The problem is that I have to get up but I don't want to."
  o "The problem is that I don't want to stop playing the computer in order to come to dinner."
  o "The problem is that my parents won't let me go out with my friends."

(3) What are my possible choices?

- The child formulates, in words, all of the different possible solutions or choices that could be made in response to the problem.
- Praise any response at this stage. Admittedly, many of the choices will sound rather stupid when stated out loud. That is the idea.
- Initially, you will have to help the child come up with some of the possible answers.
- Remember, we are seeking win-win solutions.
- Examples:
  o "I could scream that I am never coming for dinner."
  o "I could totally ignore the request."
  o "I could go have an enjoyable meal with my family. After all, mommy made me something that I like, she did all of the work, and all I have to do is come eat it. And I do have to eventually eat."
  o "I could negotiate. I'll propose that I will come up in 4 minutes. I'll set a timer so that my parents will be more likely to accept my proposal."

(4) "What is *my* choice?"

- From the possible choices in the previous step, select the best one—using words! A good choice should meet the following criteria:
  o Which choice will achieve a win-win situation?
  o Which choice is likely to be accepted by all parties?

- o Which choice is likely to work?
- Usually, ADHD children will make a pretty good choice if they have made it this far. Sometimes, they will need a little guidance. In particular, their planning for the future and their sense of timing may need some help.
- Children with Asperger's Syndrome will tend to need more instruction on the actual correct answer to a social situation. Often, they can be "scripted" with an appropriate response.
- Example:
  - o "Ignoring the request to come for dinner is unlikely to work. Mommy will eventually keep pestering me, and eventually I'll become hungry, anyway. I can't come right now because I'll lose my spot in the game if I exit at this point. Negotiate! Mommy always goes for that. Better that I come peacefully in 4 minutes than screaming which will ruin all of dinner. I'll propose coming in 4 minutes. But I better keep to the plan if I expect mommy to accept it next time."

(5) How Did I Do?

- How good was my *effort* in the problem solving process?
  - o Did I really try?
  - o Did I stick to the steps?
  - o Did I use words?
- How good was my *result*?
  - o Did I achieve a win-win situation?
  - o Did the solution actually work?

(6) Reward!!!

- This step is always positive.
- Rewards can be internal: Hopefully, the child can say to himself: "Great job!! It worked!!" Sometimes, he'll have to settle for "Nice try. Better luck next time."
- Rewards can be external: Praise whatever positive thing you can find about the process or its effort.
- Remember that we are trying to increase compliance with the process by making it more useful and pleasant. Punishment has no role here. That will only lead to avoiding the system altogether. However, good results with the system can be specifically rewarded with privileges.

Summary

Here are the steps of cognitive behavioral therapy for impulsivity:

1. Stop.
2. What is the problem?
3. What are the possible choices?
4. What is my choice?
5. How did I do?
6. Reward.　　　　Good Luck!!

Chapter 6

Practical Philosophy

Practical Philosophy

In this chapter, we leave the world of medical science and enter into the world of personal beliefs and philosophies. Some of these thoughts are taken from well-worn texts, and others are fairly novel ideas. See if any of them ring true to you. Hopefully, you will find this to be philosophy with directly practical applications. There are ideas here that we should teach to our children; the same ideas should help us deal with them.

One caveat: Often, concepts seem good, but we are just too mired in old habits, inertia, or depression to actually utilize them. This is where professional help can get a family "unstuck." To get things moving in a positive cycle, professionals can help with counseling and behavioral techniques. Physicians may also need to add medications to help with attention, impulsivity, anxiety, or depression.

Catch Them Being Good

"Catch them being good" is a deservedly popular phrase. It refers to the basic strategy of looking for the positive moments and reinforcing them, rather than focusing on the negative. For example, praise the five math problems that were completed, rather than criticizing the sixth that was skipped. Give praise for sharing the crumb at all, rather than focusing on the crumb's small size. You get the idea. It will help, if you can keep it up.

Catch Them Being Helpful: Volunteering

I would suggest that the best way to help one's own problems is to help someone else's problems instead. Many religions teach it, but *why* does the human brain work this way? I have a theory: When we teach our children to constantly focus on helping their own lives, we encourage them to view themselves as constantly deprived of something--deprived of reading ability, deprived of math ability, deprived of friends, deprived of talent, etc. Implicit in the urge to help oneself is a statement that "I do not yet have enough. I'm not satisfied yet with my life as it is. I am not happy."

In contrast, implicit in the act of helping others is a statement that "Other people have bigger problems than I do. I have enough gifts in my life that I can share them with others. I am useful. I already have enough, including a purpose in life. I am happy."

Loosely translated, helping others means volunteering. Let's encourage our children to volunteer around the house, join a volunteer club at school, join the local youth group, big brother/big sister, etc. [Note that being *forced* to help around the house may add to the child's sense of being useful, but it does not lead to the greater insight that the child already has enough to volitionally give of him/herself.]   For ideas, try:

- A Kid's Guide to How to Save the Planet
- The Kid's Guide to Service Projects: Over 500 Service Ideas for Young People Who Want to Make a Difference.

Seek First to Understand

All of us could probably benefit from adopting the stance of "seek first to understand," a phrase used in the book Don't Sweat the Small Stuff (And it's all small stuff.) Usually, we are so wrapped up in our own reaction to something that we never stop to ask: "What underlying factors made my fellow human being do that to me?" Usually, there's a good answer if we seek it out. Pausing to understand the reasons why others treat us as they do can help us control our impulsive responses. (Impulsivity is a particular problem for those of us with ADD.) Let's teach our children: First, pause to understand. Then, react.

In order to understand others better, try the following three ideas:

Life is Difficult for Everyone

M. Scott Peck's popular book, The Road Less Traveled, begins with the terse sentence: "Life is difficult." Although our children--and ourselves--often feel singled out to be victims, it often comes as somewhat of a relief to realize that we are not the only ones with problems. In fact, if you have access to this material, I think it is fair to say that compared to many people on our planet, our problems are rather small. Maybe not.

Maybe our problems *are* the greatest. Or maybe we just do not know what other people are going through. Rabbi Telushkin quotes his mother: "The only people who I know who are happier than I am are people who I do not know very well." Helping our children realize that they are not the only ones with problems may help them keep their difficulties in perspective, and may help them understand other people's points of view.

Not Everyone Sees Everything the Same

It is useful to recognize that not everyone sees everything the same. In fact, animal studies show that some of the most difficult tasks for creatures to do are:

1) Recognize that others have feelings, just like us.

2) Recognize that others may have different feelings, not just like ours.

As rarely as humans utilize the first ability, we almost never get around to the second. However, we could much more accurately come to understand the meaning of an event to our child if we recognize that their reactions may not be the same as ours. What is their reaction? Although by no means always accurate, we can open a window into a child's mind simply by paying attention to their reaction. Unfortunately, we often incorrectly dismiss their reaction by labeling it "over-reacting."

There Is No Such Thing as Over-Reacting

A psychologist I recently met taught me the following: People do not over-react. They react, by definition, appropriately to the *meaning* a situation has for them. People have "over-meanings," not "over-reactions." When our child blows up over what seems like a trivial issue to us, it may help us to understand that in our child's mind, this issue must have a tremendous amount of meaning. We could benefit from saying, "Wow, if that's how it feels to him, we better calmly discuss this," rather than "Wow, he's overreacting." For example, imagine an ADD child's tearful screaming over the process of getting dressed. He's not over-reacting. He *is* living a tough morning. Maybe that would change our reaction to his behavior. Children's "over-reactions" are a window into their minds.

Summary: First, understand. Then, react.

In short, then, we can lead our children (and ourselves) to understand other people better by teaching them to ask:

     1) "How would *I* feel in that situation?" [By simulating the situation on our own brain, we can get a rough idea of what someone else is likely to be feeling.]

     2) "How is *he* actually reacting?" [Remember that other people may approach a situation with other "baggage" than we do, and may actually react differently. Obtain a clue to another's true reaction simply by truly listening.]

We can then apply this insight to our philosophy: "Seek first to understand. Then, react."

Chapter 7

For Kids to Read:

Hey, What is this ADHD Thing, Anyway?

Kids' Chapter

What Happened to My Brakes?

Imagine this: A kid is on a bicycle speeding downhill. The world is whizzing by. He needs to avoid holes in the pavement. The road is curving. The wind buzzes in his ear, and makes his eyes tear.

Suddenly, there are rocks in the road. He goes to put on the brakes—but they don't work!! As the bike speeds downhill, just staying on it seems overwhelming. Too many obstacles call for the rider's attention. So much seems out of control. Who has time to pay attention to the huge truck coming?

That's the life of someone with Attention Deficit Hyperactivity Disorder (ADHD). It all comes from difficulty "Putting on the Brakes," to borrow the title of a wonderful book by Patricia Quinn and Judith Stern.

Here's what's happening. Your brain's "boss" is located just behind your forehead. These frontal lobes figure out where you want to go, and the individual steps of how to get there. Like any boss, a large part of their job is saying "no." For example, your parents are supposed to be the boss in your house. Think how often their job is to say "no." They're always saying things like, "Susan, do not have a fifth scoop of ice-cream," or "Bob, stop playing Nintendo so that you can do your homework," or "Jill, don't stay out past 10PM." Unless something puts brakes on our actions, we would spin out of control.

Well, at least that is how it is supposed to work. In ADHD kids, the front part of their brains—the boss—doesn't do a good job of putting on the brakes. This means that these kids may:

- Have trouble putting brakes on distractions. Their minds are pulled off the main topic by any competing action. This leads to the "Attention Deficit" of ADHD.
- Have trouble sitting still rather than checking out those distractions. This leads to the "Hyperactivity" of ADHD.
- Have trouble putting brakes on any thought that comes into their minds. There is trouble putting brakes on frustrations and over-reactions. This leads to "impulsivity."

No wonder things go out of control so often!

Why Don't I See Problems Coming?

Let's imagine another scene: Jack is in a boat, happily fishing. Reeling in the jiggling fish while still steering the boat captures all of his attention.

This is what Jack sees: This is what everyone else seems to notice:

80

Jack is so consumed by the experience of the moment (catching the fish) that he can't look ahead to see the waterfall coming up. It's not that he doesn't care about the cliff. After all, he doesn't want to fall off a cliff any more than anyone else. It's that he never gets the chance to see it. Just like the speeding bicyclist, ADHD kids often are stuck in the present moment. The future comes as a surprise. This is called a lack of "foresight." So, people with ADHD:

- Have trouble stopping long enough to consider what is best for themselves in the future. This often gets misinterpreted as not caring.
- Have trouble stopping long enough to consider what is best for other people. This often gets misinterpreted as being selfish or mean.

What other Problems Are Common for ADHD Kids?

Teachers, parents, and friends may notice many other problems for kids who have ADHD. Often, these problems are not recognized as just being part of ADHD. These kids might also:

- Be very disorganized. They often don't get the right assignments home. Even more amazing, they may do homework and then forget to hand it in!
- Find that other people seem to take forever to eat, shop, or get to the point! Time seems to move so slowly in these settings.
- Have trouble with arguing, blaming others, or even lying.
- Sometimes have "blow ups" over unimportant things.
- Yell at people who are trying to help them.
- Have trouble noticing how other people are reacting to them. After all, who's got time for that?
- Have a sense of always being nervous or worried.
- Have trouble with handwriting, or sometimes with other school subjects.

What Can We Do About It?

Hundreds of books have been written about helping ADHD. Here's some of the best advice:

- **Just STOP.** Remember, the problem in ADHD is difficulty putting on the brakes. First, we need to keep an eye out for the warning signs that our brakes aren't working—and that we are spinning out of control. The warning signs include getting angry, sensing that we are getting overwhelmed, raising our voice, and tightening our hands. When we first notice these warning signs of getting "over-heated," we then need to try extra hard to STOP. Work out a code word or phrase, such as "I need a five-minute time-out" with your parents or teachers. Go someplace quiet, such as your room. Don't worry about getting in the last words in the discussion. (You'll get a chance later.) Do something calm like reading a book, sorting cards, etc. Once you are calm, then come back for a useful discussion of the problem. Your parents should do the same thing. Sometimes, you may not notice—or may not *want* to notice—the warning signs. Then please, please, please listen to your parents when they ask you to STOP and take a five-minute break.
- **Make decisions when you are calm.** You'll be surprised how much easier it is to reach a good decision when you and your parents are calm. People cannot think clearly when they are over-excited. Returning to our bicycle example, wait until the bicycle coasts to a stop. Then, look around and calmly consider your options.
- **Realize that your parents and teachers are usually good at preparing for the future.** In the bicycle story above, your parents can be thought of as standing on the sidewalk, watching you speed downhill. Since they are not overwhelmed just trying to stay on the bike, they have no trouble looking ahead to see the truck coming. They're screaming, "Watch out for the truck!" or "Watch out for that cliff," or "Watch out for that book report due in two weeks." A parent's foresight is typically much better than that of their ADHD child. Listen to them. Please. If nothing else, it's probably fair to say that your parents usually *try* to act in your best interest.
- **Kids with ADHD typically need help with organization. Take it.** When you get older, you can hire a secretary to help you. But right now, you probably can't afford your own secretary. Do you know anyone at home that you can trust who is willing to help you for free? Teachers at school may be willing to help with organizational skills, also. Remember, it is not fair to yell at someone who is trying to help you!
- **Use physical devices for organization, such as assignment pads and timers.**
- Your doctor may prescribe medication with "stimulants" (such as Ritalin, Concerta, Adderall or Dexedrine). These medications stimulate your frontal lobes, making them perform better. Let's return to the bicycle story. Medications like Ritalin work by stimulating the stopping power of your brakes. You find yourself in less trouble because you now have a high

performance bike, which is complete with a braking system. It does not work by making you too tired to move around.

- **Read more about ADHD.**
    - o Younger children can read <u>Putting on the Brakes</u> by Patricia Quinn and Judith Stern.
    - o Teenagers can read <u>Adolescents and ADD: Gaining the Advantage</u> by Patricia Quinn.
    - o High School and college students can read <u>ADD and the College Student</u> by Patricia Quinn.
    - o Social skills—such as how to make conversations and keep friends—can be improved with the very funny book <u>How Rude: The Teenager's guide to Good Manners, Proper Behavior, and Not Grossing People Out</u> by Alex J. Packer.
- **Keep a good attitude about yourself.** Remember that ADHD kids also have many <u>great</u> traits. They know how to have fun and enjoy the present moment. They are often quite smart, very creative, and have a "why not try it?" attitude that is the envy of many people. We always need to keep in mind all that is wonderful about you.

Good luck!

Chapter 8

ADHD Summary:

Living as if There Were Only 4 Seconds Left to Live

This chapter can be given to family members and teachers.

Martin L. Kutscher, M.D.
Assistant Clinical Professor of Pediatrics and Neurology,
New York Medical College, Valhalla, N.Y.
Pediatric Neurological Associates, White Plains, N.Y.

©2003

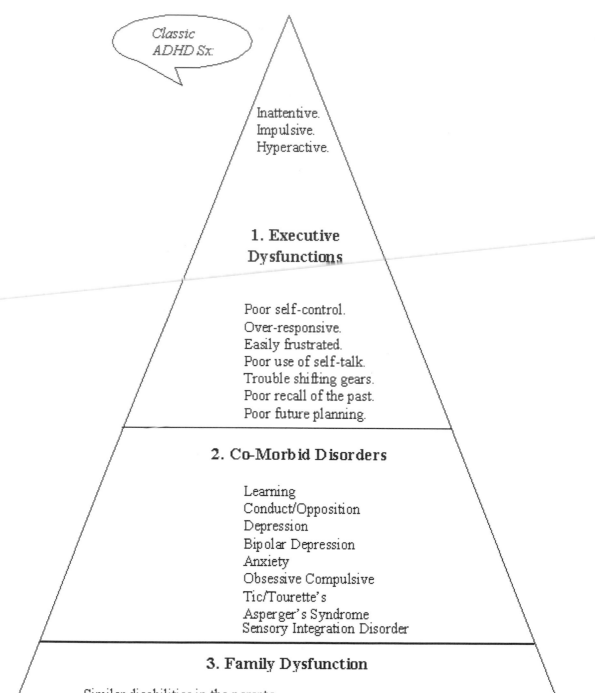

Classic
ADHD Sx:

Inattentive.
Impulsive.
Hyperactive.

1. Executive
Dysfunctions

Poor self-control.
Over-responsive.
Easily frustrated.
Poor use of self-talk.
Trouble shifting gears.
Poor recall of the past.
Poor future planning.

2. Co-Morbid Disorders

Learning
Conduct/Opposition
Depression
Bipolar Depression
Anxiety
Obsessive Compulsive
Tic/Tourette's
Asperger's Syndrome
Sensory Integration Disorder

3. Family Dysfunction

Similar disabilities in the parents.
Family stress coming back to exacerbate the patient's original problems.

ADHD BOOK: Summary Chapter

Martin L. Kutscher, MD

We've Been Missing the Point

> *"Johnny is very active! He never stops moving. He gets distracted by any little noise, and has the attention span of a flea. Often, he acts before he thinks. His sister, Jill, is often in a fog. Sometimes, she's just so spaced!"*

That is how we typically consider children with Attention Deficit Hyperactivity Disorder (ADHD). OK, not so bad. But that is often only the tip of the iceberg. Here is another likely description of the whole picture for a child with ADHD:

> *"I can't take it any more!! We scream all morning to get out of the house. Homework takes hours. If I don't help him with his work, he's so disorganized that he'll never do well. If I do help him, he screams at me. Since he never finishes anything, everyone thinks he doesn't care. No matter how much we beg or punish, he keeps doing the same stupid things over and over again. He never considers the consequences of his actions, and doesn't seem to care if they hurt me. It's so easy for him to get overwhelmed. Sometimes, he just wants to 'turn the noise off.' He is so inflexible, and then blows up over anything. It gets me so angry that I scream back, which makes everything even worse. Now that he's getting older, the lies and the cursing is getting worse, too. I know he has trouble paying attention, but why does he have all of these other problems as well?"*

It is not a coincidence that children with ADHD often manifest so much more than the classic triad of inattention, impulsivity, and hyperactivity. When we focus merely on these typically defined symptoms, we fail to deal with the whole vista of difficult problems experienced by patients and their families. This spectrum includes a wide range of "executive dysfunction" (such as poor self-control and foresight), additional co-occurring disorders (such as anxiety, depression or conduct disorders), and family stresses. These are summarized in the first figure.

Redefining ADHD as "Executive Dysfunction"

ADHD needs to be redefined to include a wide range of "executive dysfunction." As Russell Barkley explains (see Resources), this dysfunction stems from an inability to inhibit behavior so that demands for the future can be met. In other words, people with ADHD are so drawn to the present that the future does not even "show up on their radar screen." There is no future or past; only "NOW."

So, what are Executive Functions?

When you step on a snake, it bites. No verbal discussion occurs within the snake's brain. No recall of whether striking back worked in the past. No thought as to where this action will lead to in the future. No inhibition. Stepped on. Bite back. Humans, fortunately, have the option to modulate their behavior.

No single part of the human brain is solely in charge of this modulation. It does appear, however, that our frontal and pre-frontal lobes function largely as our "Chief Executive Officer (CEO)." Orchestrating language and memory functions from other parts of the brain, these frontal centers consider where we came from, where we want to go--and how to control ourselves in order to get there.

Most importantly, the ability to inhibit ("putting on the brakes") is central to effective executive function. Successful execution of a plan largely involves putting brakes on distracting activities. These brakes--courtesy of our pre-frontal inhibitory centers--allow us the luxury of time during which we can consider our options before reacting.

This lack of inhibition is a double problem for people with ADHD. First, without these brakes, they will be viewed as unable to adequately inhibit distractions, inhibit impulsive reactions, or inhibit physically acting upon these stimuli (hyperactivity). Second, patients with ADHD do not inhibit their behavior long enough for the *other* executive functions below to adequately develop either. Executive functions identified by Barkley include:

Self-talk refers to the ability to talk to ourselves--a mechanism by which we work through our choices using words. Toddlers can be heard using self-talk out loud. Eventually, this ability becomes internalized and automatic. However, ADHD patients have not inhibited their reactions long enough for this skill to fully develop.

Working memory refers to those ideas that we can keep active in our minds at a given moment. For example, in order to learn from mistakes, you have to be able to juggle not just the present situation, but also keep in mind past times when certain strategies did or did not work. Working memory hopefully also includes keeping future goals in mind (such as remembering that we want to get into a good college, not just do the most intriguing activity currently available). Without the ability to inhibit, people with ADHD never get to develop good function of their working memory.

Foresight (predicting and planning for the future) will be deficient when inadequate working memory teams up with a poor ability to inhibit the present distractions. People with ADHD cannot keep the future in mind. They are prisoners of the present; the future catches them off guard. In fact, surprisingly poor foresight is perhaps the greatest difficulty in their lives.

Sense of time is an executive function that is usually extremely poor in ADHD.

Shifting from Agenda A to Agenda B is a difficult task requiring good executive function. Pulling yourself out of one activity and switching to another--transitioning--is innately difficult, and requires effort and control.

Separating emotion from fact requires time to reflect. Each event has an objective reality, and an additional "emotional tag" which we attach to it. For example, a traffic jam may occur, causing us to be late for work. That is the objective fact. How we react, though, is up to the emotional tag of significance that we place on it. Do we stay calm, and make plans to finish up a little later. Or, do our emotions cause us to see the traffic as a personal, unfair attack--causing us to seethe and curse. Without the gift of time, we never get to separate emotion from fact. This leads to poor ability to judge the significance of what is happening to us.

In short, then, the ability to modulate behavior comes largely from our pre-frontal lobes, which function primarily as inhibitory centers. Without the luxury of inhibitory brakes, ADHD patients do not get to fully utilize any of their frontal lobe "executive functions."

What are the different kinds of problems in ADHD?

Redefining ADHD as inadequate inhibition explains a wide spectrum of difficulties experienced by people with the syndrome. This expanded spectrum of symptoms can create an environment of havoc. For more details, see the important works by Barkley, Greene, and Silver listed in the Additional Resources.

1. Symptoms of Executive Dysfunction

In the previous section, we defined the components of executive dysfunction. Now, we will translate problems in these areas into real life symptoms.

a. Classical Symptoms of ADHD

ADHD is typically defined as a triad of inattention, impulsivity, and hyperactivity. Figure 2 (see pages 109-110) is a simplified version of the DSM-IV criteria for ADHD. These are the symptoms that receive the most attention from doctors, and all come from an inability to inhibit.

- *Distractible*   <=Inadequate inhibition of extraneous stimuli.

- *Impulsive*   <=Inadequate inhibition of internal stimuli.

- *Hyperactive*   <=Physically checking out those stimuli.

b. Other Symptoms of Executive Dysfunction

If we do not address the following additional executive function issues, we are only dealing with a small part of the problem. These are not just "incidental" symptoms. They are hard to live with—ask either the patient or his family.

- *Lack of foresight!!!* ("Johnny, you'll never get into a good college if you all you do is play videogames. Why do you keep shooting yourself in the foot?") Foresight--the ability to predict the results of our behaviors--is a major adaptive ability of humans. We can run imaginary simulations of the future on our brain's computer. Lack of use of this ability can be the most

90

devastating part of ADHD. Mothers--often endowed with great foresight-- are crushed as they watch their child repeatedly head down counter- productive paths.

- *Poor hindsight/Trouble learning from mistakes* ("Johnny, how many times do you have to be punished for the same thing.") Unable to inhibit the present, Johnny cannot stop to consider lessons from the past.

- **Live at the "mercy of the moment."** **("Johnny is always swept away by whatever is happening to him right then and there.") ADHD behaviors make sense once we realize that they are based on reactions taking only the present moment into account. It is not that Johnny doesn't** *care* **about the future; it is that the future and the past don't even exist. Such is the nature of the disability. By way of analogy, imagine riding down a river with a leaking canoe. You would be so overwhelmed by the need to bail out water that you would not see the upcoming cliff. It's not that you don't "care" about falling over a cliff--it's that you don't even get to consider it.**

- *Life in the next 4 seconds.* **If you want to make sense out of inexplicable behaviors by someone with ADHD, just ask yourself: "What behavior makes sense if you only had 4 seconds left to live?" For example, if you only had 4 seconds to live, it would make sense to lie in order to expediently get out of a problem…After all, who cares about a future reputation when there is no future?!"**

- *Poor organization* ("Johnny, you never told me that there is a paper due tomorrow! And, why do I always have to go back to school for your books?")

- *Trouble returning to task* ("Johnny, you never come back to complete anything. You just don't care.")

- *Poor sense of time* ("Johnny, what have you been doing all afternoon? You can't spend one hour on the first paragraph!")

- *Time moves too slowly* ("Mommy, you are taking forever to go shopping!")

- *Poor ability to utilize "self-talk"* to work through a problem ("Johnny, what were you thinking?! Did you ever think this through?")

- *Poor sense of self awareness* (Johnny's true answer to the above question is probably "I don't have a clue. I guess I wasn't actually thinking.")

- *Poor internalization and generalization of rules* ("Johnny, why do I need to keep reminding you that playing videogames comes *after* you finish your homework.)

- *Poor reading of social clues* ("Johnny, you're such a social klutz. Can't you see that the other children think that's weird.")

- *Inconsistent work and behavior.* ("Johnny, if you could do it well yesterday, why is today so horrible.) With 100% of their energy, they may be able to control the task that most of us can do with 50% of our focus. But who can continually muster 100% effort? As the joke goes: ADHD children do something right once, and we hold it against them for the rest of their lives.

- *Trouble with transitions* ("Johnny, why do you curse at me when I'm just calling you for dinner?")

- *Hyper-focused at times* ("When Johnny is on the computer, I can't get him off. And once his father gets his mind on something, off he goes!")

- *Poor frustration tolerance* ("Johnny, why can't you even let me help you get over this?")

- *Frequently overwhelmed* ("Mommy, just stop. I can't stand it. Just stop. Please!")

- *Gets angry frequently and quickly* ("Johnny, you get flooded with emotion so quickly. Why are you always angry with me? Even though you usually apologize, it still hurts me.")

- *Push away those whose help they need the most* ("Mommy, stop checking my assignment pad. Get out!").

- *"Hyper-responsiveness"* ("Mommy, you know I hate sprinkles on my donuts! You never do anything for me! I hate you!") Barkley uses the term hyper-responsiveness to indicate that people with ADHD have excessive emotions. Their responses, however, are appropriate to what they are actually feeling. So next time you see someone "over-reacting," realize that they are actually "over-feeling," and must feel really awful at that moment.

- *Inflexible/explosive reactions* ("Johnny, you're stuck on this. No, I can't just leave you alone. Johnny, now you're incoherent. Johnny, just stay away. I can't stand it when you break things!") Greene (see Resources) goes into extensive explanation about the inflexible/explosive child.

- *Feels calm only when in motion* ("He always seems happiest when he is busy. Is that why he stays at work so late?")

- *Thrill seeking behavior* ("He seems to crave stimulation at any cost. In fact, he feels most 'on top of his game' during an emergency.")

- *Trouble paying attention to others* ("My husband never seems to listen when I talk to him. He just cannot tolerate sitting around with me and the kids. He doesn't "pay attention" to his family any more than he "paid attention" in school.") As the patient gets older, people in his life will increasingly expect more time and empathy to be directed their way. Yet, the behaviors above of ADHDers may interfere with their demonstration of these traits, despite their passions.

- *Trouble with mutual exchange of favors with friends.* Without establishing a reliable "bank account" of kept promises, friendships can be hard to make.

- *Sense of failure to achieve goals* ("Somehow, I never accomplished all that I thought I could or should have.") This deep disappointment is commonly what brings adults with ADHD to seek help.

- *Lying, cursing, stealing, and blaming others* become frequent components of ADHD; especially as the child gets older. According to some particularly depressing data by Russell Barkley, here is how ADHD children compare to typical children:

Symptom	ADHD Children (%)	Typical Children (%)
Argues with adults	72	21
Blames others for own mistakes	66	17
Acts touchy or easily annoyed	71	20
Swears	40	6
Lies	49	5
Stealing (not involving threats)	50	7

[Barkley RA, Fischer M, et al. The Adolescent outcome: An 8-year prospective follow up. Journal of the American Academy of Child and Adolescent Psychiatry, 29, 546-557.]

- In short, the symptoms of ADHD become less "cute" as the children switch from elementary to secondary schools. The "good" news comes from understanding that these problems are commonly part of the syndrome we call ADHD. They are nobody's fault--not yours, and not your child's. This understanding points the way towards coping with these issues.

2. Co-Occurring Disorders Associated with ADHD

In addition to the executive dysfunctions above, there are a myriad of co-occurring disorders which frequently accompany the diagnosis of ADHD in the patient and/or her family. These disorders may often be *misdiagnosed as* ADHD, or they may *co-exist with* true ADHD. In addition, many people are "subsyndromal," and have just parts of the following diagnosis. John Ratey (see Resources) refers to these as "shadow syndromes." The presence of these disorders must be investigated whenever the diagnosis of ADHD is being considered.

[Medications for the co-occurring disorders in children are used frequently "off-label," and information is quite limited. Recommendations need to be taken as subject to change and debate. Full discussion of the usefulness, monitoring, drug interactions, etc. of these medications is beyond this paper. The reader is referred to ADHD with Comorbid Disorders by Pliszka (see Resources), which forms much of the basis of the

following medical recommendations. Medical treatment of the associated disorders is perhaps best done in consultation with a neurologist or psychiatrist.]

a. Learning Disabilities (LD)

Twenty to thirty percent of patients with ADHD have LD. A review of the diagnostic criteria for ADHD (Figure 2 on pages 109-110) will show that an Organizational Disability is virtually built into the syndrome of ADHD by definition. Following directions, sequencing problems and dysgraphia are also particularly common. Learning disabilities should be suspected whenever a student does not "live up to his/her potential." They are identified with history, exam and psycho-educational testing. As well explained by Larry Silver (see Resources), learning disabilities can either exacerbate or mimic ADHD. After all, how long can someone focus on something that she does not understand?

b. Disruptive Behavioral Disorders

50% of ADHD children have Disruptive Behavioral Disorders. Even in the absence of a full diagnosis, the lives of many (if not most) children with ADHD are afflicted by lying, cursing, taking things that do not belong to them, blaming others, and being easily angered. This frequency is not surprising given the executive dysfunction hypothesis. Full definitions can be found in the Diagnostic and Statistical Manual-IV. Medications such as mood stabilizers (eg. Depakote, Catapres, and Risperdal) can sometimes help with impulsivity and aggression.

- Oppositional Defiant Disorder (ODD). Whereas ADHD children do not comply because of inattention or impulsivity, ODD children are unwilling to conform (even with an intriguing task). They may be negative, deliberately annoying or argumentative, angry and spiteful.

- Conduct Disorder (CD). Children with CD are more frequently overtly hostile and law breaking, with lack of remorse, not seen in ADHD alone. These people violate the rights of others, such as with physical cruelty to others or animals, stealing, etc.

- Antisocial Personality Disorder. People with Antisocial Personality Disorder have a pervasive pattern of severe violation of the rights of others, typically severe enough to merit arrest.

c. Anxiety Disorder

Anxiety Disorder occurs in up to 30% of children with ADHD, but half of the children never tell their parents! Patients are beset most days by painful worries not due to any imminent stressor. Children may appear edgy, stressed out, tense, or sleepless. There may be panic attacks or an incomplete (or negative) response to stimulants.

Treatments include:

- Change of environment, behavioral approaches; exercise; meditation.

- SSRIs (Selective Serotonin Reuptake Inhibitors) such as Prozac, etc.

- buspirone (Buspar)—helps anxiety but not panic attacks.

- clonzaepam (Klonopin)—helps anxiety.

- Tricyclics—helps some with anxiety; great for panic attacks.

- Stimulants may help if anxiety is a secondary problem, but may also worsen anxiety.

d. Obsessive Compulsive Disorder (OCD)

Obsessive thoughts and compulsive actions may occur in up to one third of ADHD patients. If ADHD is living in the present, then OCD is living in the future. Although difficult to live with, the future goal directed behavior of OCD may help overcome the organizational problems of ADHD. SSRI's are the current mainstay of medical treatment.

e. Major Depression

Depression occurs in 10-30% of ADHD children and in 47% of ADHD adults. Although pure ADHD patients get depressed briefly, they flow with the environment (changing within minutes). In contrast, depressed children stay depressed for long periods. The symptoms include loss of joy, sadness, pervasive irritability (not just in response to specific frustrations), withdrawal, self-critical outlook, and vegetative symptoms (abnormal sleep or appetite).

Treatment:

- Counseling; adjusting environment.

- Selective Serotonin Uptake Inhibitors (SSRIs) such as Luvox, Paxil, Prozac, and Zoloft.

- bupropion (Wellbutrin)—helps depression and ADHD.

- venlafaxine (Effexor)—helps depression and maybe ADHD.

- Tricyclics (e.g.: Tofranil, Pamelor) do not appear to work in children for depression in controlled clinical trials.

f. Bipolar Depression

Bipolar depression occurs in up to 20% of ADHD children. These children show depression cycling with abnormally elevated, expansive, grandiose, and pressured moods. Children may cycle within hours. Other hallmarks include severe separation anxiety and often precociousness as children; extreme irritability; extreme rages that last for hours; very goal directed behavior; and little sleep requirement. They may demonstrate hypersexuality; gory dreams; extreme fear of death; extreme sensitivity to stimuli; often oppositional or obsessive traits; heat intolerance; craving for sweets; bedwetting; hallucinations; possible suicidal tendencies or substance abuse. Often symptoms are shown only at home. See The Bipolar Child by Papolos (under Resources)

Consider bipolar when a diagnosis of "ADHD" is accompanied by above symptoms or:

- strong family history of bipolar disorder or substance abuse.

- *prolonged* temper tantrums and mood swings. Sometimes the angry, violent, sadistic, and disorganized outbursts last for hours (vs. less then 30 minutes in ADHD).

- bipolar rages are typically from parental limit setting; in ADHD, rages are from overstimulation.

- oppositional/defiant behaviors.

- explosive and "intentionally" aggressive or risk seeking behavior.

- substance abuse.

- separation anxiety, bad dreams, disturbed sleep; or fascination with gore.

- morning irritability which lasts hours (vs. minutes in ADHD).

- symptoms worsen with stimulants.

Medical treatment of bipolar depression:

- valproate (Depakote).

- carbamazepine (Tegretol) clearly helps bipolar and aggressive symptoms at least in adults (no controlled studies in children).

- lithium (not clear that it works in children who cycle so rapidly; does not help ADHD).

- Plus risperidone (Risperdal) for psychotic symptoms and aggression.

- Plus cautious use of stimulants or antidepressants for ADHD symptoms.

- Stimulants and antidepressants may trigger mania and worsen bipolar depression.

g. Tics and Tourette's (motor & vocal tics, +/- ADHD, OCD, LD)

Seven percent of ADHD children have tics; but 60% of Tourette's patients have ADHD.

Medical treatments include:

- clonidine (Catapres) / guanfacine (Tenex)—help impulsivity & tics.

- stimulants—helps ADHD but may worsen (or improve) tics.

- tricyclics—mild ADHD help but tic "neutral." Cardiac concerns.

h. Asperger's Syndrome

ADHD and Asperger's syndrome can cluster together. Symptoms include impaired ability to utilize social cues such as body language, irony, or other "subtext" of communication; restricted eye contact and socialization; limited range of encyclopedic interests; perseverative, odd behaviors; didactic, monotone voice; "concrete" thinking; over-sensitivity to certain stimuli; and unusual movements.

See Attwood's book (Resources).

i. Sensory Integration (SI) Dysfunction

SI dysfunction is the inability to process information received through the senses. The child may be either oversensitive or undersensitive to stimuli. Or, the child may not be able to execute a coordinated response to the stimuli. SI may mimic or co-exist with ADHD. SI is typically evaluated by an occupational therapist. See Kranowitz's book (Resources). Some types of SI include:

- Hypersensitive to touch: sensitive to clothes or getting dirty; withdraw to light kiss.

- Hyposensitive to touch: wallow in mud; rub against things; unaware of pain.

- Hypersensitive to movement: avoid running, climbing, or swinging.

- Hyposensitive to movement: rocking; twirling; unusual positions.

- May also respond abnormally to sights, sounds, smells, tastes or textures.

- May be clumsy; have trouble coordinating (bilateral) movements; or have poor fine motor skills.

3. Familial Issues.

This can be of two categories:

a. Family members with their own neuro-psychiatric problems

Family members may have their own ADHD, OCD, depression, anxiety, etc. In fact, a child with ADHD has a forty percent chance that one of his parents have ADHD. Such difficulties affect the family's ability to cope with the ADHD child, and may need to be addressed independently.

b. Stress--created by the child--cycling back to further challenge the patient.

Children or adults with ADHD can create chaos throughout the entire family, stressing everyone in the process. The morning routine and homework are frequent (and lengthy!) sources of dissension. Other siblings are often resentful of the time and special treatment given to the ADHD child. Mothers, who frequently consider their child's homework to be their own, find it stressful that "their" homework never seems to get completed. Fathers come home to discover a family in distress, and that they are expected to deal not only with a child who is out of control, but also with the mother who is understandably now losing it, too. Parents may argue over the "best strategy," a difficult problem since no strategies are even close to perfect. The unpleasantness of life around someone with ADHD leads to a pattern of avoidance, which only furthers the cycle of anger. *In turn, all of this family turmoil creates a new source of pressures and problems for the already stressed ADHD patient to deal with.*

Non-Medical Treatments for ADHD

First, we need to identify and treat any of the above symptoms. We need to recognize that "ADHD" is shorthand for this entire biologically based spectrum. Otherwise, parents will think that they have a child with ADHD who just also happens to be difficult and/or appear mean spirited.

Non-medical treatment usually requires academic and organizational support. Learning disabilities need to be identified and treated. Computers can help with handwriting and spelling difficulties, graph paper can help with the spacing of math problems, and clip-art can help with art projects. Organizational support includes close supervision of all tasks by parents; checking assignment pads by teachers; small, structured settings; one to one attention when possible; good eye contact; having the child repeat directions; and possibly two sets of school books (one for school, one for home).

Behavioral reward approaches can also ameliorate symptoms. Children with ADHD are like moths: they are drawn to the brightest light. Unfortunately, sometimes the brightest light is a bug zapper. Our goal is to make sure that the brightest light is a productive one. If the light is bright enough, they will go there. It is fortunate--but not an accident--that children with ADHD can be easily enticed by quick rewards. After all, they are creatures of the moment. No doubt, it would be better if the children were adequately motivated by their own internal "high ideals." But for those ADHD children who do not see how doing thirty math problems right now will lead to a better world, external rewards may be needed.

Reward systems rely on children's natural desire to please their parents. If a child's basic relationship with her parents is so full of anger and resentment that she no longer finds pride in pleasing her parents, then those basic relationships need some healing first, before behavioral modification programs are likely to be successful. Set aside a period of special time (up to 30 minutes) where the goal is simply to exist together pleasantly in the same room. The child gets to choose the (reasonable) activity, and the parent gets to enjoy being near their child without provoking a world war. Avoid saying anything critical--even if it *would* be helpful. Keep questions and comments (even positive ones) to a minimal level. After all, interruptions are still annoying. The goal here is to put your account of good/bad interactions into a positive balance, making it more likely for the child to want to please you. That sets the stage for smoother discipline in the future. Dr. David Rabiner (see http://www.helpforadd.com/behtreat.htm) and Dr. Russell Barkley (see Resources) provide a full explanation of this technique.

Typical behavioral plans are token systems which motivate via strongly enticing rewards; and if needed, by punishments. Such programs are explained in detail by both Barkley and Silver (see Resources). Barkley's guiding principles for behavioral approaches include:

- Feedback and consequences that are:

    - Immediate

    - Frequent

    - Powerful

    - Consistent

    - Preferably positive

    - Clearly defined and reviewed before difficulty arises

    - Acted upon without extensive moralizing

- Recognition that the ADHD person has a disability.

    - Do not personalize the ADHD person's actions.

    - Be forgiving to the child and yourself.

- Use tangible, physical methods to externalize problem areas.

    - Explicitly state out loud the problem and consequences at the time of the event.

- Use timers and planners to break down time into manageable, concrete tasks.

- Brainstorm ideas on index cards or word processor. Then, physically sort through and order thoughts.

Just STOP!

Some people's brains are too inflexible and explosive to respond consistently to such systems. This occurs more commonly in the pre-teen and teen years. Nothing good can come from a "discussion" held by out of control people. Once that fact is recognized, some families may be ready for Plan B: try to prevent incoherent "meltdowns" *before they occur*--by allowing a cooling off period at the first sign of their appearance. Sometimes this involves being coached or cajoled through the difficult situation. Other times, we need to be left alone to regain composure. Once cool heads prevail all around, calm discussion of the issue can productively ensue. An attitude of negotiation must prevail on all sides. Sometimes, we are better off just "picking our fights." These approaches are empathically explained in Ross W. Greene's excellent book, The Explosive Child.

In summary, STOP!!! Remember, the hallmark of ADHD is trouble stopping--trouble putting on the brakes. Thus, it is not surprising that the first step in dealing with ADHD is to STOP. You will notice that the sections on anger management, problem solving skills, and general behavior techniques all begin with the need to STOP. Only then can executive function resurface. Typically, when calm and unthreatened, even the ADHD brain will make the correct choice. The need to first STOP applies to both the child and us! See also the chapter on Cognitive Behavioral Therapy.

In addition, regular exercise is also frequently reported as useful.

Medical Treatments for ADHD

When behavioral approaches are insufficient, medication is frequently warranted; and in fact, often gives the patient the tools to successfully follow behavioral plans. Medications for ADHD usually involve the stimulation of frontal lobe function. Specifically, they increase firing of noradrenergic pathways. Remember, the frontal lobes function primarily by way of inhibition. Thus, to use an analogy, stimulants "slow you down" by equipping the bicycle with adequate brakes. Importantly, they do not work by "gumming up the gears." ADHD patients bump into less trouble because they are now a high performance bike capable of appropriate braking, not because they are too tired to get going. Stimulants allow putting on the brakes against distractions, impulsivity, over-reactions, and frustrations. They give the executive functions a fighting chance.

Stimulants

Stimulant medications are the mainstay of medical treatment for ADHD. No other class of medicine works as well or as safely. Many of the executive dysfunctions will improve, although other approaches may be needed if there are co-occurring symptoms. Although usually well tolerated, the most common side effects are insomnia, loss of appetite, and rebound irritability. Precipitation of tics, headaches, abdominal distress, and other less common side effects can also occur.

- methylphenidate (Ritalin, Concerta, Metadate CD, Focalin)

- dextro-amphetamine (Dexedrine)

- mixed amphetamine salts (Adderall and Adderall XR)

- pemoline (Cylert) is rarely used now because of potential hepatotoxicity.

Non-Stimulants

- bupropion (Wellbutrin)

    - Novel antidepressant with dopamine agonist and noradrenergic effects.

    - May decrease hyperactivity and aggression and improve cognition.

    - May precipitate seizures and tics.

- nortriptyline (Pamelor) or imipramine (Tofranil)

  - Cardiac concerns.

  - Consider if stimulants are ineffective; or with co-occurring tics.

  - Does not help any co-occurring depression in children in clinical studies.

- clonidine (Catapres) or guanfacine (Tenex)

  - Centrally acting alpha-adrenergic agonists.

  - Helps impulsivity/aggression and tics but less useful for attention.

  - Controversy over apparent safety when used with stimulants.

- atomoxetine (Strattera)

  - New once daily norepinephrine reuptake inhibitor

  - May be especially useful in patients with tics, anxiety, or insomnia.

  - More long term research needed to determine its role.

- venlafaxine (Effexor)

  - Noradrenergic and serotinergic properties.

  - Limited adult studies suggest effectiveness for ADHD.

- risperidone (Risperdal)

  - Neuroleptic.

  - Useful with co-occurring tic disorder.

  - Useful with co-occurring Intermittent Explosive Disorder.

Top Principles

1. Keep a sense of humor. Seek to enjoy, not to scream.

2. Celebrate the ADHD person's humor, creativity, and passion.

3. Hate ADHD, not the person with it.

4. You do not have a standard child. You can view the issue as a disability. Or, you can view it as wonderful uniqueness. Or, you can view it as both. The perspective of "standard," though, is not an option. This "disability outlook" will help because it eliminates blame; sets reasonable expectations thereby minimizing anger; and points the way for parents/teachers to see themselves as "therapists" not victims.

5. Recognize that attention issues in the child are only the tip of the iceberg that the whole family must address.

6. The "patient" in ADHD is the whole family.

7. Remember that children with ADHD have two time frames: "Now," and "Huh." There is no future. There is no past. There is only now.

8. Do you want to understand the ADHDers actions? Just ask yourself: "What behavior would make sense if you only had 4 seconds to live?"

9. Instead of punishing wrong behavior, set a reward for the correct behavior you would rather replace it with. Rewards should be immediate, frequent, powerful, clearly defined, and consistent.

10. Plan ahead. Give warnings before transitions. Discuss in advance what is expected. Have the child repeat out loud the terms he just agreed to.

11. Don't <u>argue; nag; or attempt unsolicited and spontaneous transplants of your wisdom</u> to your child. Instead, either a) decide that the issue is aggravating but not significant enough to warrant intervention; or b) make an appointment with your child to discuss the issue.

12. Head off big fights *before* they begin. Seek to defuse, not to inflame. When tempers flare, allow everyone to cool off. Serious discussion can only occur during times of composure.

13. Especially with teens, negotiate, negotiate, and negotiate. Parents need to model negotiation, not inflexibility. Don't worry about losing control: the parent always gets to decide when negotiation is over and which compromise is accepted. **Remember: negative behaviors usually occur because the ADHDer is spinning out of control, not because he is evil. While <u>evil</u> behavior would need to be aggressively squelched, the much more common <u>overwhelmed</u> behavior needs to calmly defused.**

14. Pick your fights. Is the issue at hand worth chipping away at your relationship with your child? Can your child really control the offending behavior at this moment?

15. Although it is not the child's "fault," he will still ultimately be the one to take the consequences of his behavior.

16. This is hard work.

17. You will make it through this; you have no choice.

18. "The children who need love the most will always ask for it in the most unloving ways." [Words of a teacher quoted by Russell Barkley.]

19. If it is working, keep doing it. If not, do something else.

20. Barkley implores you to forgive your child and yourself nightly. You didn't ask to live with the effects of ADHD any more than did your child.

21. Review this text, and others, periodically. You are going to forget this stuff, and different principles will likely be needed at different stages. A good way to remember to review is by subscription to some of the free monthly newsletters on ADHD (see resources).

22. Steven Covey (<u>The Seven Habits of Highly Effective People</u>) suggests imagining your child delivering your eulogy. What do you want him to say about you? Keep those bigger goals in mind as you choose your interactions/reactions to your child.

23. This is not a contest with your child. The winner is not the one with more points. The winner is the one whose child still loves them when they graduate from high school.

Conclusion: "Doctor, Will it all be OK?"

In summary, we miss the point when we address only the triad of inattention, impulsivity, and hyperactivity. These symptoms are only the tip of the iceberg. Much greater problems have usually been plaguing the family, but often no one has understood that the associated symptoms described above are part and parcel of the same neurologically based condition. Without this recognition, families have thought that their ADHD child also was "incidentally" uncooperative and apparently self-absorbed. Unless we recognize that these extended symptoms are part of the same spectrum, parents will not mention them; and doctors will never deal with them.

Given all of this, it is reasonable to ask: "Will this go away?" Personally, I would re-phrase the question as, "Will it be OK?" The answer can be "yes," but we must recognize that this is often the "fifty year plan." In other words, these children can be wonderfully successful adults, while they continue to work on these issues over their lifetime. Meanwhile, we "just" need to patiently steer them in the positive direction.

Finally, we must also keep in mind that some of the iceberg is fantastic and enviable. While the rest of us are obsessing about the future, or morosing about the past, people with ADHD are experiencing the present. ADHDers can be a lot of fun; dullness is never a problem. Their "Why not?" attitude may free them to take chances that the rest of us may be afraid to take. Their flux of ideas may lead to creative innovations. And most importantly, their extreme passion can be a source of inspiration and accomplishment to the benefit of us all.

It's going to be quite a ride.

Figure 2. Simplified DSM-IV criteria for ADHD

Either (1) or (2)

Six or more symptoms of **inattention**

(a) fails to give close attention; careless mistakes

(b) difficulty sustaining attention

(c) does not seem to listen when spoken to directly

(h) easily distracted by extraneous stimuli

(e) *difficulty organizing tasks*

(d) *fails to follow through (not volitional or incapable)*

(f) *avoids tasks requiring sustained organization*

(g) *looses things needed for tasks*

(i) *often forgetful in daily activities*

Six or more symptoms of **hyperactivity-impulsivity**

Hyperactivity

(a) fidgets/squirms

(b) leaves seat

(c) runs or climbs excessively

(d) difficulty playing in leisure activities quietly

(e) "on the go" or "driven by a motor"

(f) talks excessively

Impulsivity

(a) blurts out answers before questions completed

(b) difficulty waiting turn

(c) interrupts or intrudes

B. Some symptoms present before 7 y.o.

C. Symptoms in two or more settings

D. Interferes with functioning

E. Not exclusively part of other syndrome

[The symptoms of inattention have been grouped together and placed in italics by the author to demonstrate how much disorganization is built into the definition of ADHD.

Using these criteria, DSM-IV defines three subtypes of ADHD:

ADHD, Predominantly Inattentive Type.

ADHD, Predominantly Hyperactive-Impulsive Type.

ADHD, Combined type.

Chapter 9

Pop Quiz

ADHD Pop Quiz

This entertaining open book quiz is designed to test and re-enforce your understanding of ADHD. The answers are on the following page.

Questions 1-5 relate to the following <u>true</u> story:

A 13-year-old son with ADHD discovers that his bite-plate is missing from its handy container. He angrily accuses everyone else of having taken it. His mother explains the blatantly obvious fact that no one else would be interested in his used dental appliance. He continues screaming and blaming her for its absence.

1) This child is demonstrating good executive function.

   a) True.

   b) False.

2) The accusatory behavior of this otherwise bright child can best be explained by:

   a) He's not quite smart enough to comprehend that his bite-plate isn't worth stealing.

   b) He's overwhelmed by frustration.

3) Yelling back and accusing your child of behaving horribly would:

   a) Prompt him to say, "Oh, thanks for helping me see the error of my ways."

   b) Cause him to be even further overwhelmed.

4) An initial attempt at helping him solve the problem is unsuccessful. A *useful* parental response at this point would be:

a) Keep escalating the screaming match.

b) Stop, walk away, retain your composure, and resist the urge to get in the last word. Resume discussion when everyone is calm.

5) This type of outrageous behavior in your ADHD child:

a) Is a common part of the brakeless behaviors we summarize with the letters ADHD.

b) Is the result of a nasty and selfish child.

6) Your child with ADHD plays guitar all afternoon, rather than complete her college applications. You can understand this behavior by realizing that:

a) She'd secretly rather stay at home another four years rather than go to college.

b) Life with ADHD means life right now, in the present. It's not that she doesn't care about college. Rather, amazingly enough, this future event doesn't even show up on her radar screen right now.

7) ADHD is primarily a disorder of:

a) Inattention

b) Inhibition of anything but the present stimulus or thought.

8) Executive functions include all *except* the following:

a) Ability to recall--and thus learn from--the past.

b) Ability to read well.

c) Ability to anticipate and plan for the future.

d) Ability to control frustrations.

9) Your goal as parent is to:

   a) Further inflame your child's overwhelmed state, leading to a deteriorating relationship.

   b) See your role as therapist--teaching her to STOP and defuse the situation.

10) FOR EXTRA CREDIT, answer Steven Covey's question: What do you want your child to say about you at your eulogy?

Answers:

Answers to questions 1-4 and 6-9: (b)

Answer to question 5:   (a)

Chapter 10

Additional Resources

Resources for
(a) ADHD and (b) Co-existing Disorders

(a) Resources for ADHD

Internet Resources on ADHD

www.chadd.org

> CHADD (Children and Adults with
> Attention Deficit Disorders)
>
> Excellent, all-inclusive support group
> with local chapters.
>
> 800 233-4050

AD(H)D Sanctuary at www.mhsanctuary.com has excellent links. In
particular, see the Resource Page.

On-line booklet from National Institutes of Health at
www.nimh.nih.gov/publicat/adhd.htm#adhd10 on ADHD

www.ADDvance.com

> Specializes particularly in girls and
> women with ADHD. They offer a wide
> range of excellent books. In particular, see
> their books *UNDERSTANDING GIRLS*
> *WITH ADHD, Putting on the Brakes,*
> *ADD and the College Student, and Raise*
> *Your Child's Social IQ (A social skills*
> *program to help parents help their kids).*

ADDitude Magazine at www.attitudemag.com

> Electronic version of excellent print
> magazine on ADHD.

ADDed Support at http://groups.msn.com/ADDedSupport/ and
ConductDisorders.com at http://www.conductdisorders.com/

> Active parent to parent message boards.

Behavioral Treatment of ADHD: An Overview by Dr. David Rabiner at
www.athealth.com/Consumer/farticles/Rabiner.htm

ADHD: 101 Tips for Teachers at
www.dbpeds.org/articles/article.cfm?name=attentiontips.

Links on developing an IEP (Individual Educational Plan) at
www.teach-nology.com/teachers/special_ed/iep/ .

Internet e-mail Newsletters on ADHD (an excellent way to keep reminding yourself of ADHD principles of care)

www.ADDchoices.com

> Newsletter offers practical information on
> the spectrum of ADHD behaviors and
> problems.

www.ADHDnews.com

> Empathically maintained and useful
> newsletter on ADHD!

www.helpforADD.com

> David Rabiner, Ph.D. writes a very useful
> and scientifically sound e-mail newsletter.

www.ADDresource.com

> ADHD newsletter and extensive source of
> further links.

Stormwatch Newsletter at www.dixiesky.com/ADHD_Soaring/ .

> Sign up for an upbeat monthly newsletter
> on ADHD.

Print Books on ADHD

Taking Charge of ADHD; Russell Barkley; Guilford Press.

> Ground-breaking material on the nature of
> ADHD and executive functions, from the
> true thinker in ADHD.
>
> Particularly for associated behavioral,
> executive problems.
>
> Harder, less optimistic reading

ADHD and the Nature of Self Control; Russell Barkley; Guilford Press.

> More on the theory of ADHD, with some
> excellent practical advice.
>
> Fairly advanced reading for the average
> parent.

Hyperactive Children: A Handbook for Diagnosis and Treatment;
Russell Barkley; Guilford Press.

> The scientific and unbelievably extensive
> literature review of ADHD, underlying
> Dr. Barkley's concepts.

Quite advanced reading. Like most
medical "handbooks," it barely fits in your
hand.

Dr. Thomas Phelan has written a series of truly excellent books on
childhood behavior. They are actually fun to read, and extremely
useful.

All about Attention Deficit Disorder is all
about ADHD for parents and teachers.

Surviving Your Adolescents: How to
Manage and Let Go of Your 13-18 Year
Olds is particularly useful for ADHD
adolescents, who have a double dose of
foresight blindness. Especially
encouraging for ADHDer parents,
because this book describes how many
families of typical teenagers experience
difficulty similar to your ADHD teen--and
most of them seem to turn into normal
adults.

1-2-3 Magic: Effective Discipline for
Children 2-12 is not about ADHD per se,
but is an excellent way to learn about
"Act, don't yak" discipline for younger
children.

Understanding ADHD; Christopher Green and Kit Chee;
Fawcett/Columbine.

Addresses serious issues in an upbeat,
even funny, style.

A great place to start reading

Dr. Larry Silver's Advice to Parents with ADHD; Larry Silver;
American Psychiatric Press, Inc.

Particularly for associated learning disabilities.

Easy reading.

Teenagers with ADD: A Parent's Guide; Chris A. Ziegler Dendy, Woodbine House.

Optimistic and practical advice for teenagers and others.

Extensive sections on specific problems such as waking up and organization.

Extensive lists of school (and home) accommodations.

Teaching Kids with ADD and ADHD site and book by Chris Dendy at www.chrisdendy.com

Driven to Distraction; Edward M. Hallowell and John J. Ratey, Simon and Schuster.

An excellent book about ADD in adults and children.

Many parents might find themselves in this book.

(b) Resources: Co-occurring Diagnoses

Child Psychiatry Topics

Pediatric Psychiatry Pamphlets at www.klis.com/chandler/home.htm by Dr. Jim Chandler provides concise, responsible information on a large variety of conditions including ADHD, ODD, OCD, Tics, Panic, and Bipolar Disorders.

www.NeuroPsychology Central.com has excellent links on neuropsychology topics.

Mental Health Links at www.baltimorepsych.com/consumer.htm and topics are succinctly covered as part of a great psychiatry site produced by Northern County Psychiatric Associates.

Tourette's Syndrome

Tourette Syndrome Association: Lists their local chapters at http://www.tsa-usa.org

Tourette Syndrome--Plus [www.tourettesyndrome.net]

> An awesome and practical site on Tourette's, OCD, Rage, etc.

www.vh.org/Patients/IHB/Psych/Tourette/Modifications.html has specific school modifications for children with Tourette's.

"Teaching the Tiger" (by M. Dornbush and S. Pruitt) is an entire book of accommodations for Tourette's students, many of which apply to ADHD and LD students as well.

Learning Disabilities

There are many related sites and support groups. Try:

LD on Line [www.ldonline.org] is a superb resource including fair, full text, useful articles. Spend an evening there!

> Includes ADD, writing, learning, speech, and social difficulties.

> In particlar, see their corner for kids. Bookmark this site!

National Center for Learning Disabilities [www.ld.org]

> Mail: 381 Park Ave. South Suite 1401
> New York, NY 10016

> Phone: (212)-545-7510

International Dyslexia Association [www.interdys.org]

> Mail: Chester Bldg, Suite 382, 8600
> LaSalle Road, Baltimore, MD 21286

> Phone (800)-ABCD123

www.Schwablearning.org

> Valuable brief articles covering a wide range of LD and associated problems.

Specific school modifications for children with LD, ADD at www.vh.org/Patients/IHB/Psych/Tourette/Modifications.html

Bipolar Depression

www.bpkids.org is a great site on Bipolar Depression.

The Bipolar Child; Demitri Papolos; Broadway Books.

Excellent diagnostic and treatment resource.

Definitive book on the subject.

Asperger's Syndrome

Asperger's Syndrome: A Guide for Parents. By Tony Attwood.

Excellent (brief) diagnostic and treatment resource.

See also his website at www.TonyAttwood.com which includes numerous excellent articles and an Asperger's rating scale

Asperger Syndrome (The OASIS Guide); Patricia Bashe and Barbara Kirby; Crown Publishers.

Another excellent and complete resource (lengthy), written empathetically and fairly.

See also their comprehensive OASIS website/support group which formed the basis for the book at www.udel.edu/bkirby/asperger/

Books/Links on Other Co-existing Disorders

ADHD with Comorbid Disorders; Steven Pliszka, Caryn Carlson, James Swanson; Guilford Press.

Encyclopedic review of the literature on
drug and behavioral treatments.

Intended for professional use.

Your Defiant Child; Russell Barkley; Guilford Press.

For Oppositional/Defiant children by a
careful researcher and thinker.

The Explosive Child; Ross W. Greene; Harper Collins.

A must read for parents of inflexible-
explosive children who do not respond
well to typical reward systems.

Wonderfully and empathetically written.

The Out-of-Sync Child; Carol Stock Kranowitz; Skylight Press.

Diagnosis and treatment of Sensory
Integration disorders.

Makes sense out of a very diffuse topic.

Sensory Integration Dysfunction at
www.tsbvi.edu/outreach/seehear/fall97/sensory.htm has information
that is understandable and complete

Shadow Syndromes; John Ratey and Catherine Johnson; Bantam Books.

Explains that many symptoms such as
ADHD, obsessions, rage, autism, etc. can
occur at "subsyndromal" levels.

Notes: